THE 7 LOST S

Ecstasy AND SUCCESS

How to Awaken Your Hidden Power For Love and Riches

Kala H. Kos, Ph.D.

Aloha Power Publishing

IMPORTANT – PLEASE READ THIS FIRST

Although anyone may find the practices, disciplines, and understandings in this book to be useful, it is made available with the understanding that neither the author nor the publisher is engaged in presenting specific medical, psychological, emotional, sexual, or spiritual advice. Nor is anything in this book intended to be a diagnosis, prescription, recommendation, or cure for any specific kind of medical, psychological, emotional, sexual, or spiritual problem. Each person has unique needs, and this book cannot take these individual differences into account. Each person should engage in a program of treatment, prevention, cure, or general health only in consultation with a licensed, qualified physician, therapist, or other competent professional. Any person suffering from any illness of his or her sexual organs or prostate gland should consult a medical doctor and a qualified instructor of sexual yoga before practicing the sexual methods described in this book.

Printed in Canada
Aloha Power Publishing
800-15355 24th Avenue
Suite #246
White Rock, B.C.
V4A 2H9 Canada
Fax: 604-535-0249

POB 223204
Princeville, HI 96722
U.S.A.
Toll-free: 866-468-4862

Email: kala@hawaiiheart.com Website: www.hawaiiheart.com

Cover design by Ken Etheridge and Kerry Jackson.
Layout design by Lara Fisher, lara@creativesoul.ca
Cover photo by Ron Dahlquist Photography.

Self-Help / Success / Spirituality / Personal Growth
ISBN #: 0-9755146-0-1

ACKNOWLEDGEMENTS

Special thanks and undying love go to my mother, Steffi; my brother, Bob; and my dear departed teacher, Freda Samuels, for their enthusiasm and encouragement regarding each one of my projects.

With deep gratitude, I thank my friend and mentor, Dr. Serge Kahili King, who taught me the concepts and techniques through which I came to understand the Polynesian practice of Huna that comprise the bulk of this book. *Leis of aloha* go to Gloria King and Peggy Kemp, who have been steadfast supporters, constantly encouraging me to spread this valuable knowledge.

With immense appreciation and love, I thank my dear friend and editor, Deanna Brady, whose patience and skill throughout the many projects on which we have worked together have made my life and my words richer.

Mahalo nui loa to my Hawaiian *ohana,* who have shared so much heart and wisdom with me — especially to Kahu Ikaika, who has enriched my life and who has dedicated his own to the furtherance of a sovereign Hawaiian nation.

I wish to acknowledge my good friend, fellow author, and teacher of Huna, Paul Waters, for the insight, wit, and advice he provided during my ongoing adventures in writing.

No words can express the profound effect that Eckhart Tolle has had on my life and how touched I am continuously by who he is. I also wish to give recognition to the wisdom of Rajneesh, to which I was introduced through the loving teachings of Ron C. Wypkema, who has deepened my spirit simply through our association.

Heartfelt thanks go to my first Tantra instructor, Margo Anand, who opened up a new realm of possibilities within me; and to my other dear Tantra teachers and friends — the Muirs, Robert Frey and Lori Grace, Kutira and Raphael, Bodhi Avinasha, and Miriam Serman — who have inspired so much ecstasy.

Thanks also go to Bill Gladstone, whose intuition, skill, and generous spirit have guided me forward in my writing career.

Most gratefully, I thank all the people who have read my books, listened to my recordings, and attended my workshops, for they have enhanced my life profoundly.

This book is dedicated to
the two angels watching over me —
my dear father, Zvonko Kos,
who always believed in me as a writer,
and my dear friend Robert Frey,
who always believed in me as a teacher.

CONTENTS

INTRODUCTION

Curing an "Incurable" Disease

As I began to chronicle the journey that led me to the writing of this book, I realized it was crucial to explain why the title refers to seven *lost* secrets. Almost two decades ago, I stumbled across a teaching that changed my life forever for the better. That teaching had been handed down for generations by ancient Polynesian masters who were known as *kahunas.*

After Captain Cook arrived in the Hawaiian islands and Westerners began influencing the ruling chiefs, kahunas and their practices were outlawed, first by the Hawaiian monarchy, and more thoroughly after annexation by the territorial government of the United States. As a result, the younger generations were no longer taught the "secret knowledge" of healing and manifestation that has come to be called *Huna*. The older kahunas soon passed away, along with much of their esoteric lore.

Fortunately, the ancient knowledge had been preserved with great care by certain Hawaiian families and through a type of code within the Hawaiian language that described the system. Over the past several decades, this hidden code has been uncovered and resurrected, notably by the Huna scholar who became my mentor, Serge Kahili King. Huna is now taught throughout the world, particularly in Europe, and it is poised to burst onto the scene in mainstream America.

The Huna philosophy embraces seven concepts based on what we all experience when we look within to observe how our own minds interact with both the physical and spiritual dimensions of existence. The primary aim of this book is to present not only the concepts behind this marvelous system of manifestation and healing, but the actual system itself, in simple contemporary terms. I have shared a deeper understanding of this ancient knowledge, in my forthcoming book, *Aloha Power: The Hawaiian Guide to Love, Health and Wealth*.

For too long we have given over our power to the external world. So many of us have looked for love and abundance "out there" and have allowed these shadows to substitute for a deeper connection with our Source. The teachings offered here are not simply techniques for getting more "stuff" – though they can certainly be practiced for that purpose. They are ultimately designed to combine our creative power and an intimate awareness of our own consciousness in order to fashion a transformed life.

I believe we are now at a turning point in our evolution. Many of us are prepared more than ever to embark on a self-directed adventure of revelation and empowerment, an adventure that is both within us and before us. It is equally the intimate frontier and the ultimate frontier.

Through a unique set of circumstances, I was blessed to set foot on the Hawaiian path to success, known as the Way of the Adventurer. Here is my story...

Never before had I known illness intimately. Persistent pain was an unfamiliar sensation to my young body. Each day I prayed that the bus driver wouldn't pull away from the curb while I was laboring to get off the back step and onto the sidewalk. Each evening I persevered, step by step in slow motion, up five flights to my New York apartment. Night after night I lay soaking in a hot bath, trying desperately to relax my spasming muscles...

The disease had such a dramatic name: *ankylosing spondylitis*. This crippling arthritic/rheumatic condition seemed much more appropriate to an elderly person than a twenty-six-year-old, and it was already causing painful inflammation of my joints. The doctors explained that it was degenerative, progressive, and potentially fatal. They also told me there was no cure. . .

From early childhood I had a secret adventurous streak. I felt that there must be something more to life than the limited view of the world I could see from the small prairie city where I grew up. I was convinced that there were tantalizing mysteries awaiting me elsewhere. I yearned for wonder, awe, a sense of the miraculous. I just knew it existed! This is the path that led me to it:

While studying English literature at a local university, I decided to apply for a position as a flight attendant with a major airline. Although I wasn't sure I was sophisticated enough for what seemed like such a glamorous job, my strong desire to travel and a sincere love of people fueled my enthusiasm in the interview. Suddenly, at nineteen, I found myself living in a major metropolis – Toronto – and flying international routes. The world opened up dramatically as I rode on gondolas in Venice, gazed upon master-works at the Louvre and danced to the rhythms of steel drums in Barbados. It was a thrilling time of personal growth, and I considered myself highly fortunate.

As I explored the globe, however, my inner horizons also continued to expand. Eventually, I began to yearn for a deeper experience of myself. Although I had continued my education while flying, I longed for a creative outlet that my work as a flight attendant just couldn't seem to provide. After seven years, I had begun to feel the limitations of my job.

One evening a friend invited me to sit in on her acting class. I had no idea what to expect. As I watched the students practice their craft, I was so inspired that I could hardly contain my excitement. Here was an art form in which I could use all of myself – my body, thoughts, feelings, and energy – to express a living character uniquely. How could anything be more creative than that? I knew then that I wanted to study this marvelous form of self-expression.

Little did I know that I was about to encounter the mysterious workings of the universe in a way that would profoundly effect my destiny. I had come to an intersection in my life, and the road I was about to take would alter me in ways I could never have imagined.

It all began during a meal service on a busy international flight with the typical task of pulling a heavy trolley up the aisle. Suddenly, I felt a flash of intense pain in my lower back. Out of necessity, I forced myself to ignore the pain and go on with my work for the rest of the night. By the following morning, the pain was excruciating, and I couldn't even get out of bed. Apparently, this injury set the stage for my incapacity, as I was faced with the onset of a disease that began to inhabit my body. Unable to continue to fly, I now had a new challenge, as well as an opportunity to change my life for the better.

Since my usual work was out of the question, I decided to try a different direction. It wasn't long before I was attending what was regarded at that time as one of America's most prestigious acting schools, the Strasberg Institute in New York City. There, I learned the importance of becoming highly sensitized, in touch with all aspects of myself and of life.

Feeling vibrantly alive in my new awareness in spite of the debilitation of my health, I immersed myself in fascinating roles. In my study of behavior, I observed people around me and began to perceive that everyone was playing a "role" in the "script" of his or her life. Some "characters" were creating the experience of love, confidence, and prosperity; others created disappointment, fear, and poverty.

It dawned on me that each of us recreates a role everyday. I realized that we all have a hand in creating our experience, and the greatest works of art, our ultimate creations, are our individual lives!

As it happened , one weekend during a human-potential seminar, I suddenly realized that the illness I had been enduring for three long years was actually of my own creation. The power of that discovery lay in my new understanding that I had the ability to "re-create" health. I knew then that I had to take action; the alternative was to end up without a job, poor and disabled, with no hope of acting professionally.

I immediately set about to create my healing. For the next year, I learned and practiced every discipline I could find that might help my body to rejuvenate itself. I monitored myself and was mindful to acknowledge every sign of improvement. Finally, I returned to the airline administration and was sent to three medical specialists, who each examined me thoroughly. This time, there was no trace of the illness in my body – not even in my blood. I was healthy and vital once again. The specialists pronounced this seeming miracle a "spontaneous remission" – and it continues to this day, several decades later.

Such was the journey that led me on an exciting search for the inner causes of outer events.

Eventually, my search brought me to the doorway of the inner world, and when I stepped through, my life changed immeasurably for the good. That adventure left me with the indelible impression that we each create our experience of reality from the inside out. I was determined to discover how.

As my interest in the "business" of acting began to diminish, my fascination with the inner workings of human experience grew. Imagine my excitement when my search led to the exploration of an ancient science of manifestation that clearly validated my discovery. Before long, I was drawn to a beautiful Hawaiian island and down the path of the age-old Polynesian art of living known as *Huna*. This began my formal study of the art and science of making things happen. I invested myself in Huna with boundless enthusiasm, and it never lost its appeal or failed to live up to its promise.

Several years after I became a Huna *alaka'i* (a leader and minister), I was led to yet another body of ancient knowledge that also enhanced my life immeasurably. This teaching originated in India thousands of years ago, and it can be practiced alone or with a partner. It is known as *Tantra,* and it is often described as the art of "sacred sexuality," a gateway to spirituality through one's own sexual energy.

Just as I had always felt that there had to be more to life than meets the eye, I felt there had to be something more to sex than just a few fleeting moments of pleasure. Inspired yet again, I became an earnest student of Tantra, exploring the depths of love and sexual energy within my own being. Like Huna, Tantra appealed to me because of its integration of body, heart, and spirit. It enabled me to take another step into an even deeper awareness of myself, others, and my environment.

I soon discovered the power of combining the knowledge of Huna with the energy practices of Tantra to manifest positive change. I began to design and teach "Ecstasy and Success" workshops based on these elements, and I saw the profound effects these teachings had on the participants. Later, I carried the same effective practices and principles into the arena of prosperity with "The Inner Road to Riches" workshops.

That is the journey that brought me to the writing of this little book packed with large ideas. It is a very basic and simple guidebook, distilling just a small portion of the vast knowledge from each of these ancient philosophies. I chose to write it for all the people like myself who sometimes wish for a concise manual that can serve as inspiration on those days when circumstances look a bit grim, and we ask ourselves, "What's it all about?"

Through sharing these ancient teachings, I have been blessed to act as a catalyst for miracles in people's lives, and I am constantly grateful for my own good fortune. Here in "paradise," on the Garden Isle of Kauai, nature shows one and all that there are truly no limits to the beauty, abundance, joy, love, and peace that everyone can experience. Come join me on this grand adventure, and become the architect of your destiny. Choose ecstasy and success in all areas of your life. You DO deserve it!

THE 7 LOST SECRETS OF ECSTASY AND SUCCESS

Ecstasy works. Yet for a long time

it has been underemployed.

The time has come to rediscover it.

One moment of ecstasy can change your life.

— Margo Anand

1

THE FIRST SECRET:

Be Aware of Your True Nature

You are in a rich, green forest. The breeze surrounds you with the scent of leaves, and every cell of your body feels alive. It's as though the grass, the rocks, the trees, and the wind are as aware of you as you are of them. They seem to be breathing oxygen into you, infusing you with energy so vibrant that you feel both powerful and peaceful. A friend you haven't thought about in a long time comes to mind, and it's a pleasant thought. Returning home hours later, you find a message on your answering service. You hear the sweet voice of your friend, calling from thousands of miles away, wanting only to say, "Hello – just thinking of you..."

Have you ever thought of someone you know, and suddenly the phone rang, as if that person had read your mind? It's a pleasing and unexpected occurrence, isn't it? What if you were able to direct your attention to thoughts of your most cherished dreams and see them

*Ecstasy is an innate state of being,
as well as a tremendous
physical experience.*

simply come true? Imagine feeling truly empowered, connected with all aspects of yourself and with your environment. Imagine being able to manifest your desires effortlessly!

There is an innate connection between the natural state of ecstasy and the phenomenon of effortless manifestation. You may have sensed what is referred to here as *ecstasy* quite keenly when looking into the eyes of a baby. It is not synonymous with *pleasure* or *happiness*. It is not a reaction to or a result of outside events. It is that fundamental state of wonder, awe, and bliss that has been referred to as *timeless awareness*.

Assume the basic premise that ecstasy is *the nature of who you are,* that it is available to you at any moment and is not dependent on anything outside you. When you access your own inner ecstasy – which is part of Universal Intelligence – you also begin to see spontaneous positive change occur in your life.

The first key element of success, which we will define as *effective living with effortless ease*, is ***awareness***. This book will show you how to be more aware and flexible in your endeavors. You will learn how to open your thoughts, feelings, and body to become more receptive to the miraculous. Using the seven *secrets* and their associated *elements* listed in this book, along with techniques that utilize *three essential tools* for directing energy (sound, breath, and movement), you can create your own means to ecstatic ends.

Ecstasy is an innate state of being, as well as a tremendous physical experience. The more open you are to an awareness of your true nature, the longer and more frequently you will enjoy this state.

You become more loving, more charismatic,
more powerful, more peaceful,
and more successful
in every way...
with a lot less effort.

The object of this book is to learn the art of unfolding to ecstasy. It is also meant to assist you in the game of bringing the formless into form. Through a doorway of subtle energies, you begin to experience yourself in partnership with the magical forces of the universe. You learn to awaken the ecstatic reflex within yourself and realize a life of increased ease and fulfillment.

What are the practical benefits of this state? They include new vitality, enduring youthfulness, expanded personal magnetism, a deeper acceptance of self and others, a renewed feeling of innocence, enhanced intuition, more experiences of love, pleasure, and joy, a richer flow of opportunity and abundance, and an acceptance of your own vastness within each moment.

This is an extraordinary kind of living. Not only are daily stresses relieved, but these practices allow you to attract and enjoy blessings greater than you can now conceive. Incorporating these tools and secrets into your life, you become more loving, more charismatic, more powerful, more peaceful, and more successful in every way...with a lot less effort. Through their use, you will realize the magnificent and ecstatic nature of the true self!

In *The Seven Spiritual Laws of Success*, Deepak Chopra tells us:

> When you discover your essential nature and know who you really are, *in that knowing itself* is the ability to fulfill any dream you have, because you are the eternal possibility, the immeasurable potential of all that was, is, and will be...There is no separation between you and this field of energy. The field of pure potentiality is your own Self...

At those times when you find yourself
lost in discontent and unease,
notice your mental chatter,
and use the erasing motion
of your hands on your forehead
as a pattern-interrupt.

> And when you are grounded in the knowledge of your true Self – when you really understand your true nature – you will never feel guilty, fearful, or insecure about money or affluence, or fulfilling your desires, because you will realize that the essence of all material wealth is life energy, it is pure potentiality. And pure potentiality is your intrinsic nature.

Pure potentiality, your ecstatic nature, is consciousness beyond the realm of mind. To assist you in shifting out of mind and into essence more regularly, here is a simple technique taught to me by Kay Snow-Davis, author of *Point of Power, a Relationship with Your Soul.*

> Place the fingertips of both hands in the center of your forehead, and move them apart toward your temples several times, stroking lightly to release emotions and stress. After you "erase" the physical and emotional tension, command that your random thoughts STOP; then focus on moving your mental energy to your heart. (You can command your mind to "Stop and drop!" – to drop this energy downward to the heart.) Take a deep breath; then continue to focus on your breathing as you experience the power and stillness of your heart energy. In this way your mind can hear and receive truth and guidance from your heart.

> At those times when you find yourself lost in discontent and unease, notice your mental chatter, and use the erasing motion of your hands on your forehead as a pattern-interrupt. Remind yourself to "stop and drop." This will help you

The Power Breath
will charge you energetically
and relax you into the present moment.

become more aware of your own innate power, when your heart and your mind are in partnership and balance.

To experience more of your innate power in each moment, it is also helpful to turn your attention to your body and your inner energy field. According to Eckhart Tolle, the author of *The Power of Now,* "the key is to be in a state of permanent connectedness with your inner body - to feel it at all times. This will rapidly deepen and transform your life. The more consciousness you direct to your inner body, the higher its vibrational frequency becomes."

To do this, let me introduce you to a technique I call the Power Breath. It will charge you energetically and relax you into the present moment. Simply begin by noticing your breathing. Now, as you inhale, put your attention on the crown of your head, and as you exhale, put your attention on your navel. If you find it useful, place one hand at the top of your head and the other at your navel as you begin. Keep shifting your focus of attention from crown to navel with each inhale and exhale. Since *energy flows where attention goes,* the mere focus of attention on these two areas will begin the flow of energy between them. Release your hands at any point you wish, and continue the Power Breath for at least eight rounds.

You can practice this technique anytime, anywhere, with your eyes open or closed. In fact, you will find the process enhanced considerably when practiced in nature. Go for a silent walk in the woods, where there are no noisy distractions. As conservationist and Sierra Club founder John Muir said, "Nature's peace will flow into you, as sunshine flows into trees."

When you are aware of yourself as Awareness, when you are not diverting your energy with thoughts of the past or anticipating the future, you are freeing yourself from the obsession of the mind.

Keep practicing the Power Breath, and add this Witness Walk exercise shared with me by awareness facilitator, Ron C. Wypkema:

> Imagine that Existence is experiencing itself through you, and ask yourself, *What are my eyes seeing?* Spend time really seeing what is around you as you move, refraining as much as possible from analyzing, defining, or labeling anything you see. For example, *That's a beautiful tree.* Simply be the Witness of consciousness seeing. (Remember to keep shifting your attention from crown to navel with each inhalation and exhalation as you walk.) Then ask yourself, *What are my ears hearing?* and notice sounds, again without judgment or labels. Give yourself time to listen as you walk and breathe consciously. Listen to the silence beneath the sounds. Now ask the question, *What are my other senses experiencing?* Notice the air against your skin, the smells of the environment, the sensations of fabric against your body. Notice how subtly you begin to unfold to ecstasy in the moment.

When you are aware of yourself as Awareness, when you are not diverting your energy with thoughts of the past or anticipating the future, you are freeing yourself from the obsession of the mind. Life becomes full and rich. You are liberated from always striving to be better and have more.

Yet, paradoxically, as you unfold to more and more ecstasy, you notice the ease of manifesting and creating a life of your choosing. You awaken to the realization that you co-create your reality with the Universal Mind. The trick is *not to need your creations to give you a sense*

When you put your attention

on a thought, an object, or an experience,

a current of energy flows

between you and it.

of self. Rather than identifying yourself with your creations, you remain based in consciousness. You begin to notice that experiences of struggle, lack, and limitation diminish. When this occurs, it is because all aspects of your being are in a state of ideal integration.

THREE ASPECTS OF THE SELF

Think of your consciousness as expressing itself in three ways: the subconscious self, the conscious self, and the super-conscious self (also known as body, mind, and spirit). These are aspects of you as a whole, yet they have separate functions. At those times when you experience ecstasy, they are interacting harmoniously, as a team.

The manifesting of personal reality requires the cooperation of all three components of your consciousness. The super-conscious manifests your physical experience by using the patterns of your conscious and subconscious thoughts. Using the information and tools described in the following pages, you will be better equipped to harmonize all aspects of yourself and involve yourself consciously in the process of co-creating.

LIFE IS AN ENERGY EVENT

Quantum physics now confirms what the ancients have long taught: that the universe is made up of energy and consciousness. Therefore, there is no real separation in the universe, and you are connected to everything in a unifying field of conscious energy. When you put your attention on a thought, an object, or an experience, a current of energy flows between you and it. Doing this repeatedly then draws the equivalent experience to you (or you to it).

I focused all my mental, emotional, and physical resources on the idea and experience of health.

At the age of twenty-six, I had a dramatic demonstration of the truth of this principle. I was a vibrant and healthy young woman, employed for several years as a flight attendant on international routes, when I experienced what I believed was a "twist of fate." After injuring my back while working on a flight, I contracted an illness known as *ankylosing spondylitis*. I was told that it was a potentially fatal arthritic/rheumatic disease with extremely debilitating effects and with no known cure. Conventional medicine had little idea how to treat it. Unable to work, I learned to cope with ongoing pain and frustration.

After three years, special circumstances provided me with insight into why I had brought that experience into my life, as well as with the motivation to change it. Following this new awareness, I focused all my mental, emotional, and physical resources on the idea and experience of health.

Since markers of the disease had been detected in my blood, and the airline had determined that I was not physically fit to fly while that was the case, I decided to find ways to cleanse my bloodstream. I remember attending a symphony performance during which I used the inspiration and energy of the music to focus my imagination on purifying my blood. I visualized it shooting up from the center of a beautiful white fountain in front of me, cascading down in pure, opaque red. The powerful music seemed to intensify my desire and conviction. As I left the concert that evening, I felt I had taken significant strides toward health and might even have altered my own physical reality.

From that point on, I continued to direct my attention to the normalcy of my blood, affirming my wellness and

It is possible to change
the inner causes of outer events
and, thus, actually change
the outer events.

participating in every healing modality I could find that might help my body to rejuvenate itself. Finally, after a year of concentrated effort, I fully believed I had replaced illness with health...but I didn't yet have tangible proof. Then the airline for which I had worked, cautious about returning me to active duty, sent me to three specialists who examined me thoroughly. Not one of them could find a single trace of the disease in my blood or anywhere else in my body! Since that day many years ago, I have been free of the incapacitating condition that I was told might take my life.

My own experience taught me that it is possible to change the inner causes of outer events and, thus, actually change the outer events. It also taught me the power of directed attention. Since that time, I have experienced innumerable examples of the same principles at work. By sustaining your focus of attention on thoughts, images, and feelings about having what you want, you can manifest the physical equivalents of those thoughts, images, and feelings in your life!

I feel so strongly that these concepts can assist everyone in experiencing their highest possibility, that I've made this chapter available free on my website. If you'd like to share it with someone else, just go to www.hawaiiheart.com and click on the Free Stuff link.

What lies behind us
And what lies before us
Are tiny matters
Compared to what lies
Within us.

— Ralph Waldo Emerson

2

THE SECOND SECRET:

Channel Your Focus With Intention

When you start using intent – attention fixed in a particular direction with meaning and purpose – you are participating consciously in the process of creating your life. Casually fixing attention on an idea and then seeing it come back to you in form is simply a responsive event (like the phone call). It's what we generally think of as coincidence. When you have a *"why"*, a purpose, then you have intent. Intent has to do with meaningful direction – a formed, purposeful kind of energy and fixed thought.

At this point, you may be saying to yourself, "I've focused my attention on what I've wanted many times, and I certainly didn't get those things in my life!" Yes, many people have had that experience. Then, what really *is* the key to manifesting your desires?

Why do some people manifest their dreams and some don't?

WHY SOME PEOPLE MANIFEST THEIR DREAMS AND SOME DON'T

Katherine was an attractive, intelligent, and independent woman. She had been in several long-term relationships, but she had never felt she could commit to marriage. As she reached her late thirties, she began to yearn for a life-partner and decided she was finally ready to take that step.

Very soon after making her decision, Katherine met Todd. Although their connection was obviously strong, she was cautious about becoming involved with him because he was in the midst of a divorce. "I'm at a time in my life when I finally do want to make a commitment," she told him, "and I don't want to find out several years down the road that I'm with someone who doesn't want to get married."

Todd was adamant that his deep feelings for Katherine were genuine and that he had no reservations about marrying again. They quickly discovered a wonderful rapport and became the best of friends and sweethearts. After two happy years together, they made the decision to become engaged. Another year passed, and Katherine felt it was time to make their wedding plans. On the very night they were choosing the date, Todd put up an emotional wall. He still wanted Katherine, but he didn't want to be married. It was obvious to Katherine that Todd had major fears left over from a painful ten-year marriage and was not able to get past them to make another huge commitment. She felt heartbroken. Realizing that they were not moving in the same direction, nor would they be in the foreseeable future, she chose to leave the relationship. Later, she had dreams that she and Todd had actually gone through with it.

You get
what you focus on
consistently.

She dreamed that being married was an awful experience, all that she had hoped it would *not* be, and that she felt trapped.

She soon began to suspect that Todd's fear had actually been a reflection of her own. Delving into her psyche to make sense of her experience, she uncovered some severely limiting subconscious beliefs.

Not having witnessed many models of what she considered "satisfying marriages" throughout her youth, she had unconsciously come to doubt the possibility of achieving that herself. Coming from a Catholic background in which divorce was considered a sin, she had also grown up believing that even a marriage that wasn't gratifying had to last forever. That belief had instilled a deep fear that if she married and became unhappy, she would be trapped. If either partner subsequently left the marriage, she would consider herself a failure. Before her dramatic experience with Todd, Katherine had not chosen to be fully aware of her fear of the risks of marriage.

YOU GET WHAT YOU FOCUS ON

There were probably many previous instances when that subconscious fear had reflected itself in Katherine's life; however, it had remained a background focus until her experience prompted her to discover it. Her story is a good illustration of a key element in manifestation:

The thoughts and feelings you dwell on,
in full awareness or not,
form the blueprint for your experience.

*The thoughts you think
and the feelings that follow them
have an electromagnetic reality.*

The thoughts you think and the feelings that follow them have an electromagnetic reality. The focus of your attention sets up a vibration of energy in your electromagnetic field that attracts experiences related to what you focus on. You may choose to focus your attention on particular ideas, yet subconsciously you may have conflicting thought-reactions to those ideas. This conflict is the root cause of what we often label "self-sabotage."

Rooting out subconscious beliefs is not a new idea to modern science. Uncovering the effects of past programming is the basis for the field of psychology. However, psychologists aim to alter our beliefs in order to change *reactions* to circumstances, whereas the Polynesian philosophy of Huna teaches that beliefs *generate* the circumstances, not just condition our experiences of them. Our discoveries about our deeply held beliefs can enable us to change our reality.

It is your beliefs—your thoughts, feelings, attitudes, and expectations—that draw to you everything you experience in form. It's an established fact that an electromagnetic field surrounds you. It also flows through you like an electric current and actually magnetizes your thoughts and feelings so they attract forms that are like them. Every thought you think goes into this field. If you focus on an idea consistently, it becomes magnetized more strongly and, thus, has more power to attract that idea in form. How, then, can you reprogram your subconscious with new beliefs for attracting what you truly want?

It's important to note that the conscious aspect of the mind is responsible for programming the subconscious. In *Mastering Your Hidden Self,*

The magic happens as you learn
how to align your conscious
and subconscious attention
to achieve a specific purpose
while directing a clear,
continuous flow of energy
toward your intention.

Dr. Serge Kahili King, a scholar of Huna, writes, "Conscious attention is a matter of choice; subconscious attention is a matter of habit.... The power to create your own reality is limited only by your conscious or unconscious beliefs about what is possible for you to achieve or experience and your ability to focus your attention toward the beliefs you choose.... Learning to consciously decide how to direct your thinking and keep the direction of your intent is a marvelous skill because all of your experience comes from that."

The key, then, to manifesting your desires is the directing of both your conscious and subconscious attention toward a particular purpose with as little confusion and distraction as possible.

If you are satisfied with what you are experiencing, the quality of your relationships, and the amount of love, creativity, and success in your life, that's great. If you aren't, then, with the help of your vital energy, you need to shift your complete attention to a new pattern. The magic happens as you learn how to align your conscious and subconscious *attention* to achieve a specific purpose while directing a clear, continuous flow of energy toward your *intention.*

REPLACING LIMITING THOUGHT PATTERNS

Everything in the universe is composed of energy vibrating in various patterns, and your thoughts are forms of that energy. You are constantly influenced by thought patterns of your own making or those you have adopted from outside stimuli. Continuing to think the same thoughts over time "charges" those particular ideas, which form strong patterns, becoming beliefs. Beliefs that

The principal function of the subconscious is memory, and it learns through sensory experience and repetition.

become established in the subconscious mind then act to create your experience of the world.

The principal function of the subconscious is memory, and it learns through sensory experience and repetition. One of the ways in which the subconscious becomes fixed with certain attitudes and ideas is through the repetition of an idea by a figure of authority, especially when an authority is able to engender strong emotion such as fear.

In Katherine's case, the particular thought patterns about marriage that her subconscious adopted as truth, were established predominantly through the authority of her religion and instilled through fear of entrapment and of punishment for sin. Over time, the patterns became so habitual that she no longer thought of them consciously, yet they were embedded firmly enough to form the blueprint for manifesting her experience.

Many subconscious beliefs are formed in childhood from the words and examples of parents. Unfortunately, some parents have subscribed to the old-school tradition that it is effective to demean their children so that they will strive to prove their worthiness. People who, as children, were repeatedly given such messages as "You'll never amount to anything" or "Can't you do anything right?" often struggle in adulthood with low self-esteem and experience lives of lack and limitation.

The good news is that each of us can create a more satisfying reality through our decisions about ourselves and life, through our beliefs, and through the actions we choose each day. For example, the tremendously popular and outgoing comedienne Lucille Ball was actually expelled from drama school at the age of fifteen for being

Your subconscious mind craves direction.
It relies on the conscious mind
for this direction and on the
super-conscious for inspiration.

too quiet and shy. Another brilliantly successful actor, Robin Williams, was voted in school as least likely to succeed.

It is possible to change external reality by replacing limiting thought patterns. In order to do that, we must create new, beneficial beliefs, firm enough to override the old ones. In the instance of my bout with disease, I was able to replace old subconscious beliefs that were generating energy patterns of illness with a new pattern of complete health.

In truth, the subconscious mind craves direction. It relies on the conscious mind for this direction and on the super-conscious for inspiration. If you don't direct your own subconscious, it will take direction from the external world—from parents, friends, authority figures, television, newspapers, books, or other outside influences.

Herein lies the importance of Huna—the science of manifestation—because it illustrates how the aspects of an individual must work together harmoniously in order to bring the formless into form. As Dr. King writes, "The conscious mind focuses attention on something and the subconscious mind treats the focus of attention as an event and retains a memory of it. The super-conscious uses the memory as a pattern or blueprint to create an equivalent physical experience."

You have control of only one thing in your life, and that thing alone directs the immense power of Universal Energy.

The one thing over which you have control is **how you focus your attention**.

Your sustained, focused attention channels the energy of the universe into manifesting the equivalent of what you are focusing on.

As Serge King teaches, wherever you put your attention, your energy flows, and your sustained, focused attention channels the energy of the universe into manifesting the equivalent of what you are focusing on. The key element associated with this secret is ***focus***. You can create the experience of energy following focus by doing a simple exercise.

EXPERIMENTING WITH ENERGY FLOW

In order to create a physical reference for this concept, try the following technique to explore how your mind can affect the flow of energy:

> Take a deep breath, and exhale slowly. Now hold out your hand, palm facing you, with your arm relaxed. Pay close attention to your hand. Observe its size and shape. Look at the color of your skin. Now see all the lines on the palm of your hand. Focus your attention on them so intently that you could even draw them on a piece of paper.
>
> Imagine there is a dial on your palm that can measure the intensity of your concentration. The highest number on that dial is seven, and the needle is now at three. As your concentrated attention becomes more intense, the needle moves to four. Now let's move it up to five as you feel how the intensity of your concentration increases. Now imagine moving it to six. Now go to the highest number on the dial, seven, and feel the sharp focus of your attention. Hold that focus for one more minute.

*These effects are the result
of a biological energy-flow
following the path between
your mind and the object of
your concentrated awareness.*

> Now relax your hand, but leave it in front of you, and relax your focus. Put out your other hand. Do you see or feel any difference between the two hands? You may have noticed heat, tingling, or a change in color, size or plumpness in the hand on which you focused your attention.

These effects are the result of a biological energy flow following the path between your mind and the object of your concentrated awareness. You have just experienced physically how *attention energizes*.

ATTRACTING WHAT YOU WANT

The above is an example of directing a clear, continuous flow of energy. When you harbor no doubts or conflicting beliefs about your desires, the current generated by your persistent attention will literally attract what you focus on and manifest it as your reality, using your thought patterns as templates.

A good friend, Greg, told me a story that illustrates this principle in action wonderfully well:

"I had been working with an engineering company for a year, and I realized I wasn't learning anything new. I was overworked and underpaid. I desperately wanted a change; however, positions in my field, photo-voltaic engineering, are usually hard to find and hard to get.

"I decided to try a technique I had learned to help me focus on my goals. On a piece of paper, I wrote a description of the type of work I wanted. I wasn't overly specific, but I *was* definite about what would make me happy. I knew that I wanted an intellectually challenging

*Greg's continued focus,
positive expectation, and lack of doubt
led to the effortless manifestation
of his desire.*

environment where I could really learn. I also knew that I wanted to be among friendly people, so I described the atmosphere of the place.

"Each night before bed, I read this description several times. Sometimes I'd wake up in the morning to find the paper on the floor, where it had fallen when I had dozed off. I'd been doing this for a week when I noticed a classified ad that really looked interesting. Although the job qualifications were beyond my educational background, I responded anyway and was called in for an interview.

"I discovered that I had a lot in common with the interviewer, whose first love was art. I told him about my solar sculpture, which was touring the country on exhibit at that time. The meeting was a great success. Later I learned that I was hired because of my creativity and spirit, as well as my engineering qualifications. I had been chosen over fifty other applicants, many with Masters degrees and PhDs!"

Greg's continued focus, positive expectation, and lack of doubt led to the effortless manifestation of his desire.

> If you would like me to lead you through
> the exercise on Energy Flow,
> visit www.hawaiiheart.com, click on
> Keyword Search and select the Keyword:
> ENERGY.
> It is much more effective to be guided
> through the exercise personally,
> and you will be surprised at the results!

It's a funny thing about life;
if you refuse to accept
anything but the best,
you very often get it.

—W. Somerset Maugham

3

THE THIRD SECRET:

Expand Your Possibilities Through Imagination and Energy

As we've seen, both Greg and Katherine had specific goals they wished to achieve, but a major difference affected their success in manifesting their desires. The degree to which each believed that a new experience was possible for them was a determining factor in their outcomes. With her limiting subconscious beliefs about marriage, Katherine couldn't sustain an expectation of success, whereas Greg's open expectation of an ideal situation allowed the universal energy to move in surprising and fulfilling ways.

SPHERE OF AVAILABILITY

Whatever you believe is truly *possible* for you to experience right now is precisely what is *available* to you. This is your *sphere of availability,* and it is limited only by your beliefs. That is why you must upgrade your expectations.

If you create a mental picture
of your newly conceived self
and continue to hold it in your mind,
there will come a day when
you are that person in reality.

In the movie *Thelma and Louise,* the two heroines are in the car at the beginning of their weekend adventure, and Thelma is telling Louise about her husband. Thelma's description of his behavior makes it apparent that he's more concerned with his own interests than her happiness. Louise simply turns to her and says, "You get what you settle for!"

As the successful and popular talk-show host Oprah Winfrey says, "You have to move up to another level of thinking, which is true for me and everybody else. Everybody has to learn to think differently, bigger, to be open to possibilities."

You can do this by using the key element of ***imagination***. For many decades, champion athletes have been winning events by continuously envisioning themselves executing certain movements perfectly. This is the reason that world records continue to be superseded beyond what was previously believed possible. If you create a mental picture of your newly conceived self and continue to hold it in your mind, there will come a day when you are that person in reality.

In Jane Roberts' *The Nature of Personal Reality,* Seth says:

> The main image of yourself that you have held has, to a large extent, also closed your mind to other probable interests and identifications. If you think in terms of a multidimensional self, then you will realize that you have many more avenues open to expression and fulfillment than you have been using....You, as a personality, regardless of

Put yourself into physical situations that reflect the new condition or experience. Your subconscious is then able to relate more easily to a new way of being or to the objects of your desires.

> your health, wealth or circumstances, have a rich variety of probable experience from which to choose. Consciously you must realize this and seize the direction for your own life. Your imagination can be of great value, allowing you to open yourself to such courses; you can then use it to help you bring these into being.

The reason imagination can bring these new states into being is that it operates through an interesting attribute of the subconscious mind: *It cannot tell fact from fiction; it cannot tell the difference between a real event and an imagined one.* Whatever it stores as a truth – real or imaginary – the super-conscious will replicate in form.

Since the subconscious learns through sensory experience, use all your senses to imagine yourself in the situations and surroundings that support what you want in your life. Imitate people who have things, qualities, or characteristics you desire. "Mock up" the attitudes and essence you admire. Shakespeare wrote, "Assume a virtue if you have it not." The great painter Salvador Dali said, "Those who do not want to imitate, produce nothing."

Put yourself into physical situations that reflect the new condition or experience. Your subconscious is then able to relate more easily to a new way of being or to the objects of your desires. It expands its parameters of what's possible to achieve, thereby increasing your sphere of availability.

Sometimes a sudden insight shifts the way we see life and opens up our possibilities. During a human development seminar I attended when I was ill and at the height of frustration and pain, I suddenly realized

Once you have opened yourself to new possibilities, it's important to energize them with the power of your life-force.

the close relationship between mental and emotional states and physical health. Once I saw the mind-body connection, I knew that I *did* have the power to change my mind and, thus, change the state of my body. My sphere of availability expanded to include the possibility of self-healing.

Sometimes information from a source of authority provides the permission people need to open up to new possibilities. Those possibilities, when accepted, then become realities. Through the Kinsey studies of the fifties concerning female sexuality, modern women realized it was possible to be multi-orgasmic. Since then, *the percentage of women who experience multiple orgasms has almost quadrupled from fourteen percent to more than fifty percent!* The new research into male multiple orgasm (which is *not* synonymous with ejaculation, however) will undoubtedly cause a rising trend in that experience for men.

This brings us to another key element, ***energy***. Once you have opened yourself to new possibilities, it's important to energize them with the power of your life-force.

RIDING WAVES OF POSITIVE ENERGY

In *Centering and the Art of Intimacy,* Dr. Gay Hendricks puts forth a profound concept:

> After a certain point in evolution, it is necessary to use your body to flush out your higher intentions. We can only go so far with our minds, magnificent though they are. As our intentions become higher we have to learn to ride waves of positive energy inside

It takes courage to break through the limits of the past and open ourselves to higher levels of positive energy, but it's to our advantage.

> ourselves. As positive energy polishes our inner body, we have to cooperate with it by finding ways to nurture and support its flow... We believe that at this time in evolution our species is actually creating new channels in ourselves for experiencing positive energy. How to feel good naturally, without chemical assistance, is a new task in evolution.

Now you need to learn how to open additional positive energy channels.

THE FLOW OF SEXUAL ENERGY

In childhood we learned how to limit the amount of energy we expressed. It takes courage to break through the limits of the past and open ourselves to higher levels of positive energy, but it's to our advantage.

Sexual energy is a potential source of incredible power. It is the energy that gives us life – our *life-force*. Taoist Master Mantak Chia teaches that "Sexual energy, or *ching-chi* in Chinese, is one of the most obvious and powerful types of bioelectric energy." When the flow of sexual energy is strong and clear, we are at the peak of physical health and have abundant energy and strength (and vice versa). We feel happier, and our physical abilities are most efficient. Yet, in many ways – physically, emotionally, mentally – we tend to block off the flow of our sexual energy.

Since the subconscious is drawn toward pleasure and away from pain, let's focus on some of the benefits of sex. What are they? A recent study revealed that women who are sexually satisfied have better health and age more slowly. Sex increases estrogen levels and thereby fights

The key to awakening
the ecstatic response within yourself
is your awareness of your breath
while cultivating a deep, consistent
level of relaxation in your body
so that the energy can flow unrestricted.

heart disease. It boosts immunity by lessening stress. It also eases body aches and is a good pain killer and natural sedative. People with active sex lives are less anxious, less hostile, and more playful. And...sex burns calories!

The pituitary gland produces a "love hormone" called *oxytocin* that is released in the body during sexual activity. Studies show that it heightens intuition, raises performance levels in aptitude and intelligence tests, and increases creativity. This hormone can even augment athletic ability and alleviate depression.

If you don't have a sexual partner handy, don't despair. Studies have shown that oxytocin is also released during self-pleasuring and even while simply fantasizing about sex!

Sexual energy rides on the breath. Breath, feeling, and energy are entwined. Many people restrict their breath as a quick way of stopping unpleasant feelings and excess energy. The key to awakening the ecstatic response within yourself is your awareness of your breath while cultivating a deep, consistent level of relaxation in your body so that the energy can flow unrestricted. You can then learn to raise the upper limits of the amount of inner energy you can handle, as demonstrated in the following example.

THE BEAUTY MYTH

As a teenager, Bridgitte was influenced by the popular notion that it is sexy to have a trim body and a flat stomach. In public she made it a point to be aware of her profile and held in her stomach muscles until this became habitual behavior. Years later, as an adult, she

Bridgitte discovered that the habit of tightening her stomach muscles had reversed her normal breathing patterns, cutting off her ability to feel sensations fully in the genital area.

enjoyed a good relationship with her husband, Philip, but was disappointed and frustrated with her sex life. In spite of Philip's attentiveness, Bridgitte experienced infrequent and fleeting orgasms.

The two of them began to search for ways to bring more fulfillment to their lovemaking and decided to attend my Ecstasy and Success workshop. During that weekend, Bridgitte discovered that the habit of tightening her stomach muscles had reversed her normal breathing patterns, cutting off her ability to feel sensations fully in the genital area.

Along with the other workshop participants, Bridgitte was taught the Orgasmic Reflex Exercise (ORE) to bring her focus back to her breath. She needed to repattern her breathing habits and reeducate her nervous system. She immediately began to feel stimulation, not only in her genitals but throughout her body. When she began to feel these new sensations, she wondered, "Do I deserve so much pleasure?"

She became more aware of decisions she had made, through past conditioning, that she did not deserve much pleasure and that too much pleasure would mean that she was bad or "slutty." I encouraged her to put her attention daily on breathing into her belly, practicing the ORE with Philip, and using an additional technique to increase her self-esteem.

In the months that followed, she became more loving and compassionate toward herself, as feelings of guilt and shame that had lodged in the muscles of her body began to surface. She was also persistent in focusing her attention on what she wanted as she practiced the techniques. As she has told me many times since, it was well worth it!

Breath, sound, and movement,

are the keys

to connecting with the power

of your sexual energy.

CONNECTING TO SEXUAL ENERGY

Breath, sound, and movement are the keys to connecting with the power of your sexual energy.

The following exercise will allow you to access this energy and also make a deeper connection with all aspects of yourself. You will find it most effective if you practice it regularly. (Try it before using the Triple-Ace Technique for manifestation that follows later, and notice the extra power it brings to that process.)

The most important point to remember is to stay as relaxed as possible during your practice. Tension in the face, neck, shoulders, abdomen, or hips will inhibit your breathing and the flow of energy.

ORGASMIC REFLEX EXERCISE

This exercise was drawn from bio-energetics developed by Tantra teachers Lori Grace and Robert Frey: "The orgasmic reflex is a reflexive movement that occurs when you are releasing sexual energy, most often experienced at the time of genital orgasm. It is a quick, involuntary contraction of the *abdominus rectus* muscle combined with an exhalation of breath. By practicing this reflex voluntarily, you reeducate your nervous system to access orgasmic energy at will."

Among the benefits of doing the ORE for just a few minutes every day are these: it strengthens your body's energy field; it allows your body to become more comfortable with higher charges of energy; and it promotes stronger orgasms and extends their duration.

The exercise can stir up deep feelings and generate a high degree of energy.

NOTE: It is recommended that you practice this exercise for five to fifteen minutes, but no more. The exercise can stir up deep feelings and generate a high degree of energy. Please read the "IMPORTANT" message at the beginning of this book before proceeding.

THE TECHNIQUE:

Lie down on the floor with your legs bent, your knees pointing toward the ceiling, and the soles of your feet flat on the floor. Now inhale as you rock your pelvis downward, creating a little archway under the small of the back.

Exhale as you lower the small of your back toward the floor again (and even press into the floor with the small of your back), tilting your pelvis upward so that your genital area rises toward the ceiling. Do NOT lift your pelvis off the floor. Practice this movement with the breathing until you don't have to think about doing it correctly.

It is important to keep your abdominal muscles relaxed. If you are tensing your abdominal muscles as you practice the motion, press into your feet and knees as you bring your genitals upward, to assist you in moving your pelvis.

Now, while bringing your pelvis upward, make a sound as you exhale. This can be a sigh or a guttural sound, for example, but let it come easily so it doesn't interfere with the full exhalation of breath. Again, the movement of the breath and the pelvis is this: inhale/downward, exhale/upward (vocalized). Practice this combination

One of the great benefits of the ORE is the energetic charge you build, which can be used to power your goals and purpose.

until it is automatic. Think of the movement as wave-like, and allow the free motion of your neck.

To intensify the energy flow, consciously tighten your genital muscles as you bring them upward, and relax them as you bring your pelvis downward. Make sure you're not holding your breath when you squeeze these muscles. As you squeeze and bring your genitals up, exhale with sounds, fully expressing any emotions such as sadness, anger, or joy that may be surfacing. Your body will recognize this movement of your pelvis as an expressive, assertive act.

After several rounds, relax, take a deep breath, and imagine breathing the energy up your spine. Remain quiet and relaxed for several moments with your eyes closed, feeling the effects of the process.

NOTE: If you experience uncomfortable feelings accompanying this technique, realize that they may be indications of some subconscious limitations that could be undermining your capacity for creativity and ecstasy. In the event that you experience strong and disturbing emotions, do not hesitate to seek counseling.

One of the great benefits of the ORE is the energetic charge you build, which can be used to power your goals and purpose. Now that you have generated this energy, think about where you most want to direct it.

For a diagram and audio to assist you with the Orgasmic Reflex Exercise, go to www.hawaiiheart.com, and choose the Keyword: ORE.

You have to be definite with the Infinite.
The Infinite can only become definite
when you become definite.
You have to define and declare
the good you want
before you can get it.

—Reverend Ike

4

THE FOURTH SECRET:

Direct Your Energy through Clarity, Concentration and Confidence

If you understand that your physical, emotional, and spiritual energy flows in the direction of your focus, then doesn't it make sense to focus on *what you want*, not on what you *don't* want? Clarity and focus go hand in hand; yet so many people have so little of this important element, ***clarity***.

If you aren't sure what you want, ask yourself what would fill your heart with joy while empowering you to grow in skill, awareness, and contribution. Allow yourself to sit quietly and dwell on this until an answer emerges. Then imagine the new circumstance in vivid detail, using all your senses, and notice how it feels in your body. Ideally you will experience "warm and fuzzy" feelings.

Once you are clear about what you want, the trick is to keep your mind on it, in a positive frame, as much of the time as possible. Divert potential distractions. To the degree that you are distracted, your energy isn't flowing in the direction of what you want, so it takes that much longer to manifest it.

The subconscious responds more quickly to your direction when you use your breath consciously to energize or to relieve tension.

You may already be familiar with popular techniques like "treasure-mapping" and affirmation. In themselves, these techniques have no special power. They are simply tools you can use to help yourself stay focused clearly on your intention. They do this by helping you create as much visual, auditory, and emotional stimulation as possible in order to impress your subconscious mind. These kinds of techniques must be utilized frequently until you *know and feel* the new facts to be true.

This is also the purpose of making a plan to arrive at your goal. You create on all four levels of reality: spiritual, mental, emotional, and physical. On the physical level, you must clarify your goals, make plans, then take appropriate actions to carry them out.

The following manifestation process is an effective way to familiarize your subconscious self with what you want so it can generate the pattern that the superconscious (that aspect of you also called the High Self) will bring into form. As Henry David Thoreau wrote: "I learned this at least, by my experiment: that as one advances confidently in the direction of his dreams and endeavors to live the life he has imagined, he will meet with a success unexpected in common hours."

THE MANIFESTATION PROCESS

Let's begin with the Power Breath, which will charge you energetically, bring you into the present moment, and signal your subconscious mind that something important is about to happen. The subconscious responds more quickly to your direction when you use your breath consciously to energize or to relieve tension. Your conscious breathing clears the path for an effective flow of life-force energy to help bring about the changes you want.

Act to anchor this state
in your subconscious
by using symbolism.

As before, when you inhale, put your attention on the crown of your head, and as you exhale, put your attention on your navel. Keep shifting your focus of attention from crown to navel with each inhalation and exhalation. You need not attempt to bring energy in at the crown and push it out at the navel. You are merely directing your attention to each of these centers, which starts the flow of energy between them. Continue the Power Breath for at least eight rounds.

Now that your subconscious self has been alerted, and you are in a more relaxed and energized state through your conscious breathing, you are ready to begin the process.

The following manifestation process is known as the Triple-Ace Technique: Affirm, Assume, Act.

1. Affirm the outcome of your desire. Declare it succinctly in positive, pleasurable, emotional language. (For example, *I am a millionaire, and I really love it!*)
2. Assume the final result, as if it has already occurred. Imagine yourself vividly in this desired condition. Picture yourself and your surroundings in 3-D while generating "feel-good" feelings. Even verbalize the outcome for reinforcement.
3. Act to anchor this state in your subconscious by using symbolism. For example, raise your arms with hands pointing upward to the heavens, the invisible realm. On the count of three, bring your hands down into fists as you imagine pulling your invisible desire into physical reality while shouting "Yes!" Begin taking appropriate actions in the world to further your desired outcome. Make it important to you!

It can also be very effective
to give your subconscious
a name you can use
when speaking to it,
like a nickname you might
call yourself with fondness.

Do this process consistently, at least once every day. As often as possible, speak to your subconscious, recalling the new state, and tell yourself *Yes! You can do it...you can do it!* It can also be very effective to give your subconscious (your body-mind) a name you can use when speaking to it, like a nickname you might call yourself with fondness. (Remember that there is no actual separation between your conscious and subconscious mind. For that reason, choose an endearing or empowering name that does not create a sense of separation.)

Fill up your energy field with this positive programming until you identify with it completely. Then you will find your life reflecting your new circumstance.

Through this type of repetitive reprogramming, you are creating an energy-charged idea that will form a stronger pattern than that which was previously in place. The strongest of the patterns is the one that determines your image of yourself and the reality you create.

The new words, images, and feelings will support your new ideas and instill a sense of their reality in your subconscious mind. The more you focus your attention on these new ideas, the more they will seem to be true. When you convince your subconscious mind that they are true, they will be true in every way!

MOTIVATION

You may be familiar with this information about what it takes to create your life the way you want it to be, yet you may not be striving to change your old thoughts and habits, to plan, and to follow through with

You must become

more excited about succeeding

than you are afraid of failing.

action. In fact, you may be asking yourself, "Why aren't I doing those things?" "I really *want* to do them." Perhaps – but not as much as you *don't want to do them!* You'd rather do something else or think about something else because your motivation isn't yet strong enough. Maybe you're dealing with the fear of failure, or you haven't made the goal important enough. You must become more excited about succeeding than you are afraid of failing. The motivation to change has got to be stronger than the motivation to stay the same!

Motivation is the moving force; it moves you to act. Your motivation is based on the strength of your desire, which is based on the importance of what you want and your determination to achieve it. The more important the goal is to you, the more you're motivated to go for it.

CONCENTRATION AND DESIRE

When you really want something, you tend to concentrate your attention on it intensely until you get it. You are employing another key element, ***concentration***. To concentrate is to think persistently and clearly about your objective. You then experience the results of your most dominant and consistent thinking – in other words, you get what you concentrate your mind on most often and most intensely.

A prime example of this comes from the Oscar-winning film *Kramer vs. Kramer,* which starred Dustin Hoffman and Meryl Streep. It dramatically illustrates the power of heightened concentration. The film is about a major transition in the life of a man whose wife leaves their marriage unexpectedly. Because the emotional strain and the additional demands of caring for his son

One of the most powerful factors
in bringing ideas into form
is the intensity of the desire.

disrupt his work, Ted Kramer is fired from his position as art director at a major advertising agency.

He then learns that his estranged wife, Joanna, is suing him for custody of their son, Billy. Wanting very much to keep his child, Ted hires an attorney who tells him that if he's unemployed, he has no chance of winning the case. In desperation, he manages to make a last-minute appointment with a small ad agency on the last working day before Christmas. Though the head of the agency is obviously impatient to begin his vacation and reluctant to hire someone so overqualified, Ted's intense desire and sheer determination land him the job.

The more important the goal, the stronger the desire. One of the most powerful factors in bringing ideas into form is the intensity of the desire. *Kramer vs. Kramer* is a perfect example of the power of increased concentration, motivation, and desire. Devotion to his son made Ted Kramer's goal urgently important. Concentrating his attention intensely on his goal — to care for and be with Billy — moved him to take every available action and overcome every apparent obstacle.

Since the intensity of your desire is so important, how can you increase it? Make the end result, the goal, more important by *deciding* to give it importance through your own personal authority. This desire — the passion about it, the fierce determination to achieve it — is not the same feeling as a yearning, which implies the idea of wanting something you feel you don't deserve or cannot get. Rather it is the kind of feeling that says, "*This is what I intend, and so it is!*"

Building your desire to achieve your goal will build your motivation. You can amass so much energy this way that when you concentrate your attention, it has

*The less SDUF you have in your life,
the more confident you are.
The higher your state of confidence,
the greater the flow of available energy.*

much more power. Greater motivation will help you increase your concentration of attention on obtaining the outcome you desire. You can also use reinforcement tools, such as affirmations and pictures, to keep your sights on the goal and inspire positive feelings.

This level of concentration will tighten your focus, which gives you the power to change your reality. Another effective way to increase the accuracy and consistency of your focus is by increasing the element of ***confidence***. It's important to remember that where there is less doubt and fear, there is naturally more confidence. Therefore, the best way to elevate your confidence is by finding practical ways to deal with doubts and fears. After all, doubts and fears will only increase stress, which greatly limits both your energy and effectiveness.

THE PATH TO CONFIDENCE

You have already learned that a current of energy is generated between you and wherever you put your attention. An effective way to increase the energy current between you and your goal is to remove any resistance.

The primary cause of resistance is SDUF: Stress, Doubt, Unhappiness, and Fear. When these are not present, your confidence level is high, and your desires can manifest effortlessly.

Notice the events in your life that seem to unfold easily and the skills and talents you demonstrate without much effort or strain. These things generally have very little SDUF related to them (like the phone call from the friend you thought about).

The less SDUF you have in your life, the more confident you are. The higher your state of confidence, the greater the flow of available energy.

Choose an attitude and a posture
appropriate to this state,
and practice them as often as possible.

REPLACING SDUF WITH CONFIDENCE

What can you do to optimize the state of confidence? Here is a technique for replacing SDUF with strong and positive new beliefs. This technique, known as a SDUF-Buster, prepares you for a new reality. It also allows you to project your intentions to others physically, and they automatically respond to your new self-image. Through your new body language and other subtle means of communication, others read your increased confidence and automatically feel more willing to cooperate with your clear intent.

1. Become aware of the condition or experience you would like to change (for example, fear, anger, depression, illness, poverty).
2. Acknowledge whatever you are feeling in regard to the condition or experience. Tap your breastbone slowly with your fingertips, at a point about a hand's-width down from your clavicle bones, while saying *I deeply love and accept myself even though I... (...have fears about... or ...am experiencing...).* This technique engages the thymus gland while stimulating the immune system, relieving stress as you reprogram the subconscious with your words.
3. Now, declare the positive opposite of the state or circumstance you have been experiencing (change *fear* to *courage*, *anger* to *happiness, depression* to *enthusiasm*, *illness* to *health, poverty* to *abundance.*) Use all your senses to imagine yourself in the desired state. How does it feel, sound, smell, taste? Choose an attitude and a posture appropriate to this state, and practice them as often as possible.

*Negative attitudes
can produce inner stress,
which translates as muscular tension.
This stress directly inhibits
the flow of your energy
and can even make you
physically ill.*

4. Since the subconscious works best with symbols, pick a symbol that represents the new state or condition, and carry a picture or drawing of it in your wallet or purse, or put it someplace where you will see it frequently.

Through this form of repetitive reprogramming, you will notice an improved energy flow. Negative attitudes can produce inner stress, which translates as muscular tension. This stress directly inhibits the flow of your energy and can even make you physically ill. To change your energy, change your attitude.

To be guided through the Triple-Ace Technique at www.hawaiiheart.com scroll to the Keyword: ACE. For the SDUF-Buster, select the Keyword: SDUF.

If you keep on saying
things are going to be bad,
you have a good chance
of being a prophet.

—Isaac Bashevis Singer

5

THE FIFTH SECRET:

Charge Your Intent with Positive Expectation and Emotion

Let's observe how you relate to yourself, others, and the universe through your thoughts, feelings, and imagination. What are some of the energy-charged ideas that affect your attitude?

Think about your body. Do you like it? What do you say most often about it to yourself and others? *My body is so flabby. Im so overweight. I look terrible. The older I get, the less attractive I am.* What images of yourself do you create?

What kinds of things do you tell yourself that hurt your self-esteem? Do you imagine yourself saying or doing something foolish and feeling humiliated? Do you find yourself thinking negative thoughts such as: *I'm so dumb; I never get anything right; Nobody likes me; I'm not educated enough* or *I'm just lousy at managing money*?

*Negative suggestions or statements tend to
increase your fears, anxieties,
and self-doubts,
whether they come from you
or from external sources –
from other people
or from media such as television.*

What do you tell yourself about other people, life, and the world around you? Do you sometimes have thoughts like these? *You can't trust most people. Life is a struggle. The world is not a safe place. Rich people are snobs. You have to work hard for every penny. Money corrupts. Sex is dirty. A good man (woman) is hard to find.* These kinds of ideas are so common that they can begin to sound like truths...but they're not.

Did you notice that just reading some of these statements made you feel uneasy? Negative suggestions or statements tend to increase your fears, anxieties, and self-doubts, whether they come from you or from external sources – from other people or from media such as television.

The power of words is illustrated in the astonishing book from Japan, *Messages from Water,* by Masaru Emoto, which shows the world's first pictures of frozen water crystals. The fact that water appears the same to our eyes, no matter what its qualities, piqued Emoto's curiosity to discover whether there is a difference in the information that each form of water holds. He was also curious to discover whether there was a way of seeing the differences. He conjectured that if he froze water and took a picture of the crystals that formed, he could obtain information about the water. Emoto found that the vibrations of music and words affect water more than any other factors.

His photographs based on various experiments with water are astounding. The pictures are remarkable examples of the effect that positive and negative statements exert on water.

If you accept negative statements
and suggestions,
they can adversely affect
your health, your emotions,
and your self-confidence.

Emoto divided a water sample into two parts and placed them into glass bottles:

"We then pasted a paper on one bottle that had 'Thank you' typed on it. On the other bottle we put 'You fool'. We then left them both that way for one night. The next day we froze this water and took pictures of the crystals that formed."

Basic distilled water and the words "Thank you" formed an exquisite, well-balanced crystal. The photograph is awe-inspiring. On the other hand, the water that had the words "You fool" pasted on the container overnight appeared to have reacted negatively. The basic hexagonal structure of the crystal appeared broken into grotesque pieces. Witnessing the symmetrical beauty or destruction of a crystal throughout various experiments, Emoto discovered that "good music and kind words...exert a positive effect on water."

You appear on earth physically for the first time as a fertilized egg made up of about 95% water. Floating effortlessly in the fluid of the womb, you move in rhythm with your mother's body while liquid sustenance flows into you through the umbilical cord. As an adult your body is comprised of about 70% water, just as the earth is covered 70% by water. Doesn't it make sense that the vibrations of music and words would have an effect on the water in your own body?

The point here is that if you accept negative statements and suggestions, they can adversely affect your health, your emotions, and your self-confidence.

How many times have you noticed the disempowering lyrics of a song replaying continually in your head (for

Get in the habit of paying attention to what you're thinking, hearing, and saying.

example, "I can't live if living is without you")? Accepting negative thoughts makes people SAD: Sick, Angry, and Depressed. You can choose to reject them and their influences.

COUNTERACTING NEGATIVE SUGGESTIONS

You don't have to accept negative suggestions or allow them to program your subconscious mind. Here is a way to counteract them:

First, get in the habit of paying attention to what you're thinking, hearing, and saying. Second, whenever you become aware of a negative thought or statement that might act as a suggestion, say to yourself, aloud or silently, *"Delete"* or *"Cancel that!"* It helps to visualize a cancellation sign – a circle with a diagonal line running through it. You can reinforce the cancellation by saying "cancel" to yourself several times and by taking a deep breath.

The third step is to replace the negative idea with a positive statement that affirms the opposite of the original one – a statement that you want to believe is true (even if you don't yet believe it). Say it aloud or silently to yourself. If the original suggestion was accompanied by a strong negative emotion, see yourself surrounded with white light, and imagine that this field of light has the power to dissolve and neutralize any negativity.

This method also works beautifully for counteracting unwanted suggestions from others. Silently delete or cancel any criticism directed at you, and praise yourself with a statement of the positive opposite. Neutralize any negative feelings by imagining yourself within a sphere of white light that harmonizes the energies around you.

If you find that you are putting out negative vibrations through remorse, regret, anger, resentment, shame, or guilt, don't put out more by being angry at yourself for doing that.

In this way you are focusing on harmony rather than reinforcing the idea that you need to protect yourself.

In order to have a consistently positive attitude, you must be diligent about neutralizing negative suggestions and focusing on positive thoughts and desires. This is not because "negative" thoughts, suggestions or beliefs carry more power than beneficial ones do; no one thought has more power than another. It is simply a matter of surrounding yourself with thought vibrations that are more effective for materializing the type of life you desire so that they may solidly replace the old programming. Ideas that have been accepted as true by your subconscious mind are the ones that form your reality, and it's your choice to replace ideas that limit you with those that benefit you.

Thoughts that are negative (meaning *ineffective* for the results you wish to produce) spawn negative feelings and translate into negative vibrations. If you find that you are putting out negative vibrations through remorse, regret, anger, resentment, shame, or guilt, don't put out more by being angry at yourself for doing that. First, choose to acknowledge that you are having the feeling, and witness it without judging. If it is a mild feeling, you can imagine wrapping it in a ball of light and sending it out into the universe, telling your High Self to handle it for you. Then choose to focus on some of your own positive traits, and praise those instead of demeaning yourself.

If you are stuck in a strong emotion, acknowledge it, and move your attention inward to meet it fully. You need neither repress nor indulge it but, rather, summon the courage to go into the heart of it and feel it fully. This *must* be done without allowing your mind to get

Look for the good in yourself and others...

and if you can't find it,

invent some!

into a story about it. The story will only keep you from feeling it fully and will promote an indulgence that prolongs the suffering. If you raise your courage and give yourself the time and space to focus on the feeling without *thinking* about it, it will simply dissolve. You will discover an inner peace. To expand that sense of peace even further, you may wish to step out in nature and practice the Witness Walk exercise from Chapter One.

Look for the good in yourself and others...and if you can't find it, invent some! People tend to respond to others in kind. You'll see people reacting to you in a more positive fashion. Since everything is connected energetically, others will pick up your thoughts subconsciously and begin to respond to you in a new way. By choosing consistently to discover what is good about yourself, others, and the world, you are projecting a vibration of joy and success that further reinforces that reality.

DE-STRESSING THE WORKPLACE

The workplace often presents its own unique challenges to our intentions to experience harmony and happiness. When there are difficulties in this arena, I suggest a technique that has been very effective for turning unhappy situations into happy outcomes. It requires the use of your imagination and the directing of your focus in a specific way. First, be willing to assume that all things are connected and interdependent as part of a living system, and second, assume that what you imagine within this responsive system has its own ability to influence.

Having said that, I would like you to imagine yourself surrounded with a sphere of light. If you want, you can

Choose what feels good to you, understanding that there is no right or wrong way to interpret the colors.

choose to give this light a particular color, depending on the result you desire. For instance, you could use pink for friendliness or love, green for cooperation or healing, blue for calming or confidence. Choose what feels good to you, understanding that there is no right or wrong way to interpret the colors. What matters is what feels best and is most suitable for you.

Now you can imagine this light responding to your direction and focus. Begin to expand it outward to permeate the environment and the people around you. If you like, imagine the light filled with particular patterns, soothing sounds, loving feelings or sensations.

Now, mentally or verbally, state with deep desire that the light is indeed having the effect that you want. For instance, *"The people in my workplace are cooperative and harmonious."*

Here are some examples of the positive effects of this exercise, with slight variations, illustrating the limitless possibilities in which you can apply your own creativity.

Jesse, an engineering designer in his early sixties, tells how effectively this technique worked for him at his office in Los Angeles:

"During the beginning stages of my spiritual search, I experimented with ways of establishing harmony. Physical interaction wasn't very effective because I was still answering criticism with anger. At a Huna lecture, the speaker suggested that I send loving light to influence a troublesome coworker. Since I associated pink with love, I envisioned him surrounded with a pink aura. I also incorporated genuine feelings of love. After I had done this a few minutes a day for three days, my coworker

The more positive and consistent

your thoughts,

the greater your influence.

began to display a surprisingly happy disposition, yet he couldn't account for his new harmonious attitude. We eventually became good friends!"

Another example comes from Paul, who was working in marketing and sales for a Chicago company:

"Every morning as I arrived in the parking lot, I would envision a green light around the building in which I worked. Along with the light, I used the phrase *'Harmonize the energies between us.'* As I entered the building, I sent the light to all four corners and said, *'Harmonize the energies around me.'* A feeling of calmness would come over me, and the day always started out on a positive note. It worked equally well when I met and talked with business associates and during times when I felt tension in the air."

As you can see by the results, this method has exciting possibilities for inviting more joy into everyday situations. Since we are all connected, it is possible to influence others in beneficial ways and to improve conditions at home, at work, and within the larger environment.

It is not possible to control others against their will by doing this; however, the more positive and consistent your thoughts, the greater your influence. The reason for this is simply that the subconscious minds of all individuals move toward pleasure and away from pain. Therefore, other people will be drawn to cooperate with your loving thoughts.

This concept may bring up the question of using a technique like this to impose negative suggestions or influence others negatively. People who attempt this consistently soon find themselves weakened energetically

When you criticize or curse another,
your subconscious takes it personally,
feels attacked, and draws in
its life-force energy,
thereby weakening you.

and eventually experience very debilitating effects. This is because the subconscious experiences itself as part of everything in the universe.

When you criticize or curse another, your subconscious takes it personally, feels attacked, and draws in its life-force energy, thereby weakening you. You then have less energy to manifest your own dreams. I have demonstrated this repeatedly with my students through applied kinesiology, or muscle-checking. Whenever I ask volunteers to inwardly criticize their own behavior or that of someone else, the arm that we are testing instantly becomes weak. This holds true even when that person criticizes an inanimate object (for example, "I hate money") or an organization (such as the IRS).

To restore energy flow and strength, I simply ask the participants to think of behaviors that they like in themselves or others. I ask them to praise these behaviors simply by saying *"I like that"*; and when we muscle-check again, they are stronger than ever. This demonstrates to them the power of praise (also known as *blessing*) to counteract the effects of criticism. In the mid-eighties in Los Angeles, I purchased a frame for my license plate as a reminder to whoever might be driving behind me. Above the plate was the phrase *"Look for the Good"*. Below were the words *"and Praise It"*.

In *Messages from Water,* one of the most beautiful and well-balanced shapes is seen in a crystal formed from water in a container labeled: Love/Appreciation. Emoto wrote: "Indeed there is nothing more important than love and gratitude in this world. Just by expressing love and gratitude, the water around us and in our bodies changes so beautifully. We want to apply this in our daily lives, don't we?"

Another key to success
is the positive expectation
that your desire is already being fulfilled.

To enjoy the benefits of heightened life-force energy and more harmonious relationships, focus your attention with appreciation in the moment. In disagreements with others, remind yourself to look for what *does* work and to deal only with the current situation, rather than persisting in bringing up the past. By choosing to keep your focus on the present, you are not diverting energy through thoughts of the past or the future.

THE POWER OF POSITIVE EXPECTATION

Another key to success is the ***positive expectation*** that your desire is already being fulfilled. I've learned to focus my attention with positive expectation in many situations in my life, such as in helping people magically manifest their dreams, and I am constantly delighted to witness the miraculous outcomes of my students. If you expect the worst, you are energizing that particular idea. Why not simply expect the best?

Positive expectation is supremely important in directing energy. To help you to remind yourself to expect the best, here is an acronym I learned that you can use throughout the day: EWOP – Everything's Working Out Perfectly.

You can EWOP everything. Whenever you find yourself focusing on SDUF (stress, doubts, unhappiness, or fears), just think of the word *cancel* or imagine a cancellation sign, and then *EWOP* it! Tell yourself that you can stop worrying because *everything's working out perfectly, and I don't even need to know how.* This is an opportunity to trust your High Self to bring about the desired events in the best possible way. You can give yourself an emotional break from agonizing over outcomes. When you are more relaxed, you will also be less reactive and more effective.

*The High Self is an aspect of yourself
and is therefore not
outside and separate from you.*

The High Self is an aspect of yourself and is therefore not outside and separate from you. It is said that the center of consciousness of the High Self is in a subtle body so large that its center is above our physical head. Perhaps this will clarify why it is spoken of as though it were above an individual.

EWOP EXERCISE

Think about something in your life with which you have a concern. Now decide to turn this situation over to your High Self to handle the details. Say silently or aloud, *"High Self, I'm turning this over to you. I trust you to take care of it."* Allow yourself to let go of trying to control it and just let it be.

Now, inhale with your attention at the center of the earth, and exhale with your attention in the heavens. With each ensuing exhalation, imagine that the problem, challenge, or difficult emotion is being released to your High Self to be resolved.

To the full extent of your current ability, begin to expect that the best outcome is already happening. Have confidence that everything is working out perfectly. You will do whatever may be appropriate to do in the future, but right now you can just settle back and trust that everything is turning out beautifully. This helps you to remain in a calm and clear state of positive expectation more of the time. (It's also good to remember that, while Everything's Working Out Perfectly, it also may be working out quite differently from the limited possibilities you may be imagining.)

By consciously generating positive emotion, you can increase your life-force energy exponentially.

POSITIVE EMOTION

Both positive attitudes and positive expectation generate another key element —***positive emotion***. The energy of positive emotion can break through all kinds of blocks, overriding existing beliefs that can interfere with the manifestations you desire. By consciously generating positive emotion, you can increase your life-force energy exponentially.

Earlier I spoke of directing energy to a given result. Now we're emphasizing the building up of such a strong force that when you direct your attention, it has greater power. The more energy you have available when you focus, the stronger the effects of that focused energy. One of the best ways to build your energy is through enthusiasm and excitement.

Henry Ford credited the powerful emotion of enthusiasm as one of most important factors in achieving success. One way to generate strong, positive emotion is to be very enthusiastic about the benefits of your dream or desire. This enthusiasm actively motivates your subconscious to cooperate with you in achieving your goal, precisely because of a behavior pattern I referred to earlier that often *appears* to sabotage your wishes.

Another acronym that has recently become popular best describes the basic idea that engages and motivates the subconscious: WIFM — What's in It For Me? Whatever you do, there is always some subconscious benefit in the doing of it. For some people, there are even benefits (however well hidden from the conscious mind) to being poor or being a failure. There may be an idea hidden in the subconscious mind that it is dangerous to be rich or that only bad people succeed. Whatever your

Through your enthusiasm and expectation, you can instill a new subconscious pattern that will reward you with remarkable external results.

subconscious is doing, it is doing for a perceived benefit. It may seem as though it is sabotaging your efforts, yet it is really trying to help by always moving toward perceived pleasure and away from perceived pain!

If you want to change your subconscious attitudes and behaviors quickly, dwell upon the benefits and the pleasure of the change. What are the benefits of experiencing your ecstatic nature consistently rather than fleetingly? What are the benefits of creating a life of your own choosing? What are the benefits of abundance? If you would like greater financial abundance, can you conjure up feelings of pleasure around having all the money you want in order to do everything you want to do?

Psyche yourself up! Consciously allow yourself to be emotionally excited and enthusiastic. Feel how much fun it's going to be to have and do those things. Dwell on the satisfaction and the rewards of having achieved your goal. Use mental rehearsals to see and feel yourself enjoying those benefits now! Be willing to do this every day. Using your emotions to raise your vibration in this way will literally pull you toward prosperity and success.

Through your enthusiasm and expectation, you can instill a new subconscious pattern that will reward you with remarkable external results. In many cases, it takes approximately twenty-one to twenty-eight days to change an old subconscious pattern. That's why I teach a 28-Day Formula in my workshop called *The Inner Road to Riches: Dare to Create Love, Health and Money,* that requires only ten minutes each day to imprint the subconscious self with a cherished desire. The success stories on my website attest to the astonishing results that are possible.

The time to begin focusing
on joy in your life
is now!

BRINGING JOY INTO DAILY LIFE

Focusing on joy will bring more joy into your life. My friend Jwala, a teacher of Tantra, suggests in her book *Sacred Sex* the following exercise to release more creative, joyful energy. Once you complete this exercise, you may be very surprised to find just how miserly you have been in allowing yourself the things that fulfill you. The time to begin focusing on joy in your life is now!

I highly recommend that you take the opportunity to do this exercise and the follow-up that she advocates. Also deliberately choose some activities that are childlike. *Be* a carefree child again. Step out of your adult mind-set to experience your innocence and aliveness.

1. To begin, take a look at your top ten turn-ons in life. Make a list of the things that totally absorb you when you do them – that make you lose track of time and space. These are the things that give you the most satisfaction, that keep you in the moment so you are not thinking about the past, the future, or what's for lunch. Write down the things that bring you joy, contentment, fulfillment.
2. Now prioritize the things on your list in the order of their importance to you. Which one is the most essential in your life? Which one is next? ...and so on.
3. After you have put the list in order, write down how many hours every week you spend doing each of the things on your list. If you are like most people, you will find you are not spending much time, if any, doing most of the activities on the list. If you're feeling some frustration and discontent, could that be part of the reason?

Do at least one thing

on your list every day.

Treat yourself.

Celebrate!

Once you determine what turns you on, do it (so long as it brings no harm to yourself or another), no matter what obstacles may lie in your path. If you love to paint, paint. If you like to swim, do it. If you love to play sports or ride horses or take long baths, make sure you create the space to do those things. Do at least one thing on your list every day. Treat yourself. Celebrate! As you do these things more often, a sense of inner satisfaction grows, and you become more content and begin to glow. In this state you become a fuller cup and eventually overflow. You become less needy and more able to give love.

To be guided through the EWOP exercise at www.hawaiiheart.com, pick the Keyword: EWOP. For the Top Ten Turn-ons choose the Keyword: JOY. To learn about the incredible power of praise, select the Keyword: BLESSING.

Sex energy is the creative energy
of all geniuses.
There never has been,
and never will be
a great leader, builder, or artist
lacking in this driving force
of sex.

—Napoleon Hill

6

THE SIXTH SECRET:

Enhance Your Magnetic Attraction

Joy and ecstasy are inherent to your nature, which also has at its disposal an infinite supply of energy. You will find that the more joy you experience, the more energy will be available to you. The more energy you have available to you when you focus, the stronger the effects of your focus and the better the results you can produce. This is one of the greatest benefits of experiencing the ecstatic state. You will also find that you are more magnetic to others when your energy is heightened.

CREATING CHARISMA

Not only does *energy flow where attention goes* but, conversely, *attention goes where energy flows*. When our senses are stimulated by intense energy in any form, the source of that stimulation attracts our attention. This attraction occurs in response to loud noises, bright lights, strong aromas, pungent flavors, and other such stimuli (all of which are powerful emanations of energy.)

We tend to be attracted

to some individuals

because they project powerful energy.

Similarly, we tend to be attracted to some individuals because they project powerful energy. This attractive form of energy is often referred to as *charisma* or, another key element, ***magnetism***.

Marilyn Monroe is definitely associated with the phenomenon of sexual charisma. In fact, she was able to turn this characteristic on or off at will. In her book, *Marilyn: Norma Jean*, Gloria Steinem relates the following:

> Actor Eli Wallach is one of many colleagues who remembers her sitting completely unnoticed in a room, or walking down the street, and then making heads turn in sudden recognition, at will. "I just felt like being Marilyn for a moment," she would explain.

In the perennial bestseller *Think and Grow Rich,* Napoleon Hill writes, "A teacher, who has trained and directed the efforts of more than 30,000 salespeople, made the astounding discovery that highly sexed men are the most efficient salesmen. The explanation is that the factor of personality known as 'personal magnetism' is nothing more nor less than sex energy. Highly sexed people always have a plentiful supply of magnetism. Through cultivation and understanding, this vital force may be drawn upon and used to great advantage in the relationships between people."

The following is a technique for enhancing your personal magnetism by increasing your energy field through focused breathing. It is similar to the Power Breath, but in this case you shift your attention between the crown of the head and the genital area rather than

As the electrical current of energy flowing through you increases, the magnetic field around you increases.

the crown and the navel. As the electrical current of energy flowing through you increases, the magnetic field around you increases.

The Charismatic Breath can be done anytime and anywhere. You need not close your eyes; simply focus on the shifting of your attention while standing in those dreary bank lines, while shopping for groceries or while driving the car.

1. First, simply notice your breathing. For women, slowly and consciously inhale through your nose and focus your attention on the top of your head. As you exhale through the nose, move your focus of attention down to your genitals. Continue this, shifting your focus back and forth from the crown of the head to the genitals with each inhalation and exhalation. Men, reverse the process: inhale with attention at the genitals and exhale with attention at the crown.

2. Once you feel the relaxing effects of this process, imagine that the electromagnetic field that surrounds you is increasing with each exhalation. You may even want to see this field as a cloud of light or color that expands with every outflow of breath.

This exercise can be continued for any length of time you like. Be sure to pay attention to physical sensations. For example, you may feel a tingling in various parts of your body or a current of energy moving through your spine. This is perfectly normal and only means your sensitivity to the accumulation of life-energy is increasing. This awareness is immensely valuable to your self-development.

Anyone can expand sexual charisma and use that energy effectively.

NOTE: To magnify the effects of this technique, you might go through the process silently, with eyes open or closed, while at the gym using repetitive-exercise equipment. The added physical stimulus is highly impressive to the subconscious mind.

Anyone can expand sexual charisma and use that energy effectively. If you have concerns about attracting people whose attentions you would rather not attract, direct your subconscious to attract only those who are in harmony with your highest good. Choose to direct this part of yourself with images and feelings of safety and security, regularly reinforcing the idea that the world is a safe place. Request that your High Self guide you to harmonious situations, and then learn to tune in to your intuition more frequently.

HARMONIZING RELATIONSHIPS

It is possible to improve your relationships with others through the use of conscious breathing. All of the exercises work best when you are most relaxed, so always take a few moments first to instruct your body to release tension wherever you become aware of it.

It is most effective to experience the following guided imagery with your eyes closed.

1. Close your eyes and focus on your breathing. Inhale with your attention at the crown of the head, then exhale with your attention at the soles of your feet. Repeat this process at least eight times, until your breathing is slow and even. Visualize the merging of the universal energy entering through your crown with the earth energy flowing up through your feet. Know that as you exhale they flow together throughout your

*Remember that everything
in the universe is interconnected.
Therefore, your focused intention
to harmonize yourself with others
will bring about positive change.*

entire aura, expanding it and extending it outward into the room around you. Be aware of your body. Notice any sensations of warmth, tingling, or relaxing muscles. Now focus on your inner power. Notice that you are feeling more confident and grounded in the present moment.

2. Take this feeling into a relationship you currently have. Imagine bringing into your energetic field the form and essence of a spouse, friend, work associate, lover, child, parent...or even yourself. Envision your relationship with this person, and change it for the better. See and feel harmony between you. Hear yourself praising and acknowledging this person, and feel him or her responding with acceptance and appreciation. Imagine a cocoon of green, healing light enveloping both of you. Enjoy the moment. Now, take a deep breath and say to yourself, *"I am now in harmony with...."* Complete with a closing word or phrase such as *"So it is."* Take another deep breath, and open your eyes.

Know that you can draw on this feeling anytime you wish. For the greatest effect in improving a relationship, it is recommended that you practice this exercise privately in its entirety once a day. Remember that everything in the universe is interconnected. Therefore, your focused intention to harmonize yourself with others will bring about positive change.

This exercise is also effective in harmonizing a past relationship that needs completion. For instance, if you have unresolved emotions with a past partner or a parent (who may or may not be alive), and you feel these could be blocking the manifesting of a new partner, I recommend doing the exercise with that person in mind.

Begin by building up
your inner charge of vital energy
while repeating specific statements
so that you're more highly empowered
to accomplish your intent.

ATTRACTING YOUR IDEAL MATE

If you so choose, it is also possible to use focused breathing with intent to magnetize your ideal mate to you. It's counterproductive to visualize a particular face or body. Instead, go fully into your feelings of love and passion, desire and longing, eagerness and joy. Bring your whole being into the state of pure love for yourself and for the person you seek. Let your ideal mate feel your love intensely!

Remember to enlist the help of that aspect of yourself most directly connected to the Universal Intelligence – your High Self – by turning over the selection process to that part of you.

Trust that this wise component of who you are truly knows all the necessary characteristics of the person who is best suited to you. As the great poet, Rumi, has said: "Lovers don't finally meet somewhere. They are in each other all along."

The following is a variation of a magnetizing exercise that appears in my book *Aloha Power: The Hawaiian Guide to Love, Health and Wealth.* In it, you begin by building up your inner charge of vital energy while repeating specific statements so that you're more highly empowered to accomplish your intent. Then you focus on your heart as you accept your new love into your life.

*You will be repeating messages of self-love
and love for your approaching mate
while focusing your attention
at your heart.*

1. As you inhale with your focus at the crown of your head, say to yourself, "*I am receiving love*," and feel the universal energy flowing into you.

2. As you exhale with your focus at your navel, say to yourself, "*I am sending love*," and imagine your love flowing out to your sweetheart.

3. Continue with this receiving/charging procedure for at least eight breaths.

Now, with this raised charge and ongoing flow of energy, you will be repeating messages of self-love and love for your approaching mate while focusing your attention at your heart.

1. Inhale with your mind quiet and your focus at the the crown of your head.

2. As you exhale with attention at your heart, say to yourself, *"Here I am – I love myself!"*.

3. With your mind quiet, inhale as these words resonate through your being.

4. Exhale with attention at the heart, saying, "*I accept you in my life – I love you!*".

5. Repeat at least eight times, or as long as it feels appropriate. Then stop and quietly enjoy the afterglow.

Through regular repetitions,
you are establishing an energy link
with the person who is
in resonance with you
on the deepest levels.

Through regular repetitions, you are establishing an energy link with the person who is in resonance with you on the deepest levels. Your success will rest on how powerfully you desire the results and how often you return your attention to this process with utmost confidence.

It's also valuable to consider why you long to attract a mate. Many people look for a relationship to remedy feelings of loneliness or worthlessness, hoping that someone else can give them what they feel inadequate to give themselves. The partner may temporarily meet the need for love and acceptance. However, as Eckhart Tolle's says in his little book *Practicing the Power of Now:*

> Love is a state of Being. Your love is not outside; it is deep within you. You cannot lose it. It is not dependent on some other body, some external form... If you continue to pursue the goal of salvation through a relationship, you will be disillusioned again and again. But if you accept that the relationship is here to make you conscious instead of happy, then the relationship will offer you salvation, and you will be aligning yourself with the higher consciousness that wants to be born into the world.

Visit www.hawaiiheart.com and find the Keyword: HARMONY, to hear the exercise for Harmonizing Relationships. For Attracting Your Ideal Mate, select the Keyword: MATE.

In reality, we are divinity in disguise,
and the gods and goddesses in embryo
that are contained within us
seek to be fully materialized.
True success is therefore
the experience of the miraculous...
When we begin to experience our life
as the miraculous expression of divinity—
not occasionally but all the time —
then we will know the true meaning
of success.

— *Deepak Chopra*

7

THE SEVENTH SECRET:

Connect with Cosmic Intelligence through Meditation and Forgiveness

You have now come a long way on the path of ecstasy and success. With awareness, you have learned how to direct your focus and energy toward a desired result through increased clarity, concentration, confidence, and positive expectation. You have also learned to use breath, sound, movement and imagination as well as positive emotion to build up the force of your vital energy. Then, when you direct your focused energy, it has greater power.

You are now able to direct the three aspects of yourself—the conscious, the subconscious and super-conscious—as partners in the art of creation. You have also taken steps to experience how your body can know pleasure, your mind can know happiness, your heart can know joy, and you may even have had a taste of how your entire being can know ecstasy.

You may encounter something on your path, however, that is a major inhibitor of the ecstatic state.

Stress

is antithetical

to the ecstatic state.

This impediment has become more prevalent in recent years with the full-blown onslaught of the Information Age. This culprit cannot only deplete your energy and fray your nerves, it can also reduce your life span. The culprit's name is *ongoing stress*. It is the result of accumulated tension in the body.

We know that continuous stress causes disease. It over-stimulates the heart and weakens the immune system. In women, it can interfere with the reproductive system by disrupting the hormonal balance. Over the past fifty years, research has shown that stress even quickens the aging process. Equally as significant, stress undermines confidence, and it is the state of ultimate confidence that correlates with effortless manifestation.

When you are in stress mode, your coping skills are diminished. The buildup of tension in the body interferes with your memory, feelings, and awareness. The more this repression occurs, the more fear is engendered within the subconscious, for it begins to experience a sense of separation that leads to insecurity. Fear and doubt arise, rather than confidence. The fear mode leaves no room for inner guidance and wise decision making. The conscious and subconscious are thrown into disharmony. As you can see, stress is antithetical to the ecstatic state.

However, there is one mind-body method that can alleviate the stress response directly. According to *Time Magazine*, this method is one thing that Goldie Hawn, Shania Twain, Heather Graham, Richard Gere, and Al Gore have in common with ten million other people in the United States. This key element is known as ***meditation***.

Many people profess to have difficulty in meditating consistently. For those who do rise to the occasion and

One of the greatest benefits

of meditation

is a reversal of the aging process!

practice regularly, there are exquisite benefits: an improvement in health and vitality, strengthened coping mechanisms, as well as access to inner guidance and profound inspiration. However, one of the greatest benefits of meditation is a reversal of the aging process! The research two decades ago by physiologist R. Keith Wallace indicated that meditation has profound rejuvenating effects on the body.

According to Deepak Chopra in *Ageless Body, Timeless Mind:*

> Beginning in 1978, Wallace researched the effects of meditation on human aging. He used three markers for biological aging as shorthand for the aging process as a whole: blood pressure, near-point vision, and hearing threshold, all of which typically decline as people grow older. He was able to show that all these markers improved with long-term practice of TM [a form of meditation], indicating that biological age was actually being reversed. Meditators who had been practicing the TM technique regularly for fewer than five years had an average biological age five years younger than their chronological age; those who had been meditating longer than five years had an average biological age twelve years younger than their chronological age. These results held good for both younger and older subjects.

Certainly the lowering of biological age is a fabulous benefit! Yet there is another even more significant benefit.

"The Zone" refers to that state of stillpoint,
or pure potentiality,
at the integrated core of our being
from which arises
all effortless manifestation.

THE STILLPOINT ZONE

The process of meditation serves as a vehicle to create a strong, harmonious rapport between the three aspects of self that opens the pathway to fantastic abilities. Perhaps you have heard the term *"the Zone"* used by athletes or others who have achieved feats of exceptional accomplishment. *The Zone* refers to that state of *stillpoint,* or *pure potentiality,* at the integrated core of our being, from which arises all effortless manifestation.

It is no wonder that Phil Jackson, praised as the greatest basketball coach of his era, instructed the Los Angeles Lakers in the art of meditation and insisted that they practice regularly. He was undeniably aware that this routine was instrumental in their success.

When you relax into the state of stillpoint, and your skills correspond with your new beliefs and expectations, you witness *instant* success. Occasions of so-called "mysterious coincidence" increase, and you find yourself in awe of the seeming "miracles" that unfold before you.

WHAT IS MEDITATION AND HOW DO YOU PRACTICE IT?

One dictionary definition states that to meditate is to engage in contemplation. However, as the enlightened master Rajneesh explained:

> Whenever you can find time for just being, drop all doing. Thinking is also doing, concentration is also doing, contemplation is also doing. Even if for a single moment you are not doing anything and you are just at your

*In beginning a meditation practice,
you may discover that it opens up
an intimate relationship with yourself
that is very deep.*

> center, utterly relaxed – that is meditation. And once you have got the knack of it, you can remain in that state as long as you want; finally you can remain in that state for twenty-four hours a day...
>
> So meditation is not against action. It is not that you have to escape from life. It simply teaches you a new way of life: you become the center of the cyclone. Your life goes on, it goes on really more intensely - with more joy, with more clarity, more vision, more creativity - yet you are aloof, just a watcher on the hills, simply seeing all that is happening around you. You are not the doer, you are the watcher. That's the whole secret of meditation, that you become the watcher.

In beginning a meditation practice, you may discover that it opens up an intimate relationship with yourself that is very deep. Since it is unfamiliar territory, you may find yourself avoiding it. However, if you choose to stay with the practice, your rewards will be great. You will begin to experience more frequent states of ecstasy in the midst of your everyday routine, and you will be amazed at the countless instances of unfolding miracles — especially if you take time to dwell briefly on a goal or intention before you begin your practice.

In order to establish a new subconscious habit pattern, it is often recommended that you set up a meditation schedule. The best time of day to meditate is when you can be free of interruption and distraction. You may want to experiment with different times to see which is optimal for you.

*The repetition of shifting your focus
will lead your mind out of
its normal thinking process and
into the silent gap between thoughts.*

Once you set a specific meditation time, maintain it no matter what. You will then become accustomed to being silent at those times, and you will find the practice easier. If you are a beginner, and you wish to meditate consistently, begin with ten to fifteen minutes each day. Eventually you may wish to increase that to twenty or thirty minutes, either once or twice a day.

Meditating for an hour a day is a worthy goal. Goldie Hawn, who has been meditating for thirty-one years, reportedly practices thirty minutes, twice a day. However, do not let a suggested time frame deter your practice. Even a few minutes of meditation, a few times a week, is better than nothing.

You may find that your experiences during meditation range from ordinary to extraordinary; from boredom to bliss. Don't worry about doing it right, and let go of your expectations about what *should* happen — just be the witness.

THE STILLPOINT EXERCISE

I have found it advantageous to begin with a stillpoint exercise before your meditation. By bringing you to your calm center, this step prepares you to remain in a meditative state more easily. From the stillpoint exercise, you will transition into a simple meditation technique. With this method, the repetition of shifting your focus will lead your mind out of its normal thinking process and into the silent gap between thoughts. Don't try to force anything to happen or to chase your thoughts away in an effort to make your mind blank. Simply breathe deeply while bringing your focus back continually to the inhalation and exhalation. To begin, set aside a period of undisturbed time for this process.

Be aware of the air moving in and out of your nostrils.

Be seated with eyes closed, spine upright, and hands turned palm up, resting comfortably on your lap. Simply turn your awareness to your breathing. Take a deep breath, and hold it for five seconds. Then exhale, and remind yourself to *relax*. Be aware of the air moving in and out of your nostrils.

Focus on your dominant hand.

Simply pay attention to that hand.

Now begin to focus on both hands simultaneously.

Begin to focus on the top of the head.

Now shift your focus to about
an inch above your head.

Focus now about an inch in front of your forehead.

Focus now about an inch in front of your throat.

Focus now about an inch in front of your chest.

Focus now about an inch in front of your navel.

Focus now about an inch in front of your pubic bone.

Focus now about an inch behind your tailbone.

Center your focus on your dominant hand once again,
and allow the energy to build.

Begin to focus on both hands as you fill them
with the energy created by your conscious attention.

Begin to focus again at the top of the head,
and feel this triangle of energy.

Now relax your focus, and keep your eyes closed.

Return your attention continually to each inhalation and exhalation.

THE STILLPOINT MEDITATION

With your eyelids still closed, allow your eyes to turn slightly upward. Put your attention on your breath, and notice it becoming more rhythmic. Now begin to shift your focus as follows:

1. As you inhale, place your attention at the crown of your head.

2. As you exhale, place your attention on both upward-facing palms.

3. Feel the triangle of energy that builds with each breath. When thoughts come into your awareness, release them and continue to focus on your inhalation and exhalation. When you wish, shift your attention from your crown to an imaginary point three feet above your head, inhaling with attention at that point and exhaling with attention at the palms.

At any time, you may wish to try another powerful form:

1. With eyes closed, focus at mid-point between your eyebrows. When you are at that point, your eyes will become fixed. Relax your face, your jaw, your entire body. Now imagine a dot at this point.

2. Notice that you are seeing the dot – and notice that there is a witness in you which is seeing you seeing the dot.

Enjoy the experience of silence;
enjoy the energy and peace
generated within you.

3. You may find that thoughts are moving before you as if on a screen. You are not identifying with these thoughts, merely witnessing them. Simply continue to hold your attention there, at the "third eye," and relax into the delicate vibration of your breathing.

4. Enjoy the experience of silence; enjoy the energy and peace generated within you. When you are prepared to come out of this state, return with an attitude of gratitude for all the good in your life. Now, take a deep breath, and open your eyes.

Ground yourself by looking around the room and noticing particular colors, shapes (for instance, circles or squares), and the spaces between the shapes. Let yourself integrate this experience for several moments before returning to your regular routine. Notice how you feel. James Powell wrote, "In receptivity we are capable of opening to radiant gardens of energy."

If these simple practices feel effective for you, continue with them. If you feel that they don't suit you, be flexible, and try a different method. There are many forms of meditating, and there will be one that suits itself perfectly to your own needs. Just persevere until you find it!

NOTE: If you find your mind particularly active at a certain time and your thoughts are especially bothersome, take a few moments to do a technique called Alternate Nostril Breathing. It assists in calming the mind. You will be amazed at how much easier it is to stay centered when you again return to meditating. To find out how to do this practice, see the instructions at the end of the chapter.

Practicing a form of meditation
on a regular basis
is one of the most loving things
you can do for yourself.

A RETURN TO LOVE

Meditation is one of the oldest known paths human beings have taken to explore realms of experience beyond the conscious self. Practicing a form of meditation on a regular basis is one of the most loving things you can do for yourself. As you quiet your mind, you are better able to sense subtle energies and sensations in your body and, thus, expand your ability to experience pleasure. Practicing meditation and then bringing that calm and focus to your interactions with a partner is also one of the finest gifts you can give in a relationship.

By taking time to be at peace, in quiet connection with your breathing and with your inner being, you are able to attune with cosmic Intelligence. This is your opportunity to be guided to great acts of creativity and high states of love.

The spirit of love, the "aloha spirit," is embedded within the cultural and spiritual traditions of the Hawaiian islands and uniquely distinguishes them on the planet. Another translation of *aloha* is "the joyful sharing of life-energy in the present." Such sharing requires letting go of negative feelings from the past or projections into the future that might interfere with joyfulness or disrupt inner peace in the present moment.

The ancient Hawaiian masters were very aware of the significance of energy exchange. Knowing that the universe works through a harmonious interaction of giving and receiving, they understood that the sharing of loving energy was a way to come into attunement with divine power. They called on the High Self and aligned with cosmic Intelligence to bring forth their manifestations. But first they would release any guilt,

You may wish to assess any
blame, resentment, anger, or guilt
that may be blocking the doorway
to the good fortune you desire
and then commit
to releasing it wholeheartedly.

anger, or resentment that might stand in the way of aloha.

Releasing was always a crucial first step, for if there was any blockage of energy by these emotions, this would disrupt the outcome. With great reverence they undertook to make a ritual of releasing anyone who they felt had done them any injustice or to whom they had done an injustice. The only sin in the Hawaiian tradition was to harm another person intentionally. Holding a grudge against anyone was so disruptive to the harmony of the family that a person who refused to give up a grudge would be exiled from the family.

Many spiritual teachers understand the powerful effects of love and inner peacefulness in implementing desired outcomes. Kahu Ikaika, a Hawaiian advocate and teacher, guides others through a beautiful "clearing" visualization that is meant to be practiced before beginning any manifestation process. Hawaiian elder, Ed Kaiwi, frequently emphasizes "never to take anything personally," to become vigilant about "not being offended."

You may wish to assess any blame, resentment, anger, or guilt that may be blocking the doorway to the good fortune you desire and then commit to releasing it wholeheartedly. This brings us to the final element, ***forgiveness***, both of yourself and of others. I would suggest that you create your own "forgiving and releasing" ceremony, since ritual is very impressive to the subconscious self. We use rituals such as weddings, grand openings, applause, blind dates, birthday parties, and funerals constantly in our lives. Such ceremonies are done to impress the subconscious of the participants or to help focus our attention.

So much more
than material wealth and success –
even more than what you normally
perceive as love –
can be yours as you awaken
to your true self.

A particular ritual I believe can be highly effective is based on the process of completing a Radical Forgiveness Worksheet, taken from a profound book called *Radical Forgiveness, Making Room for the Miracle*, by Colin C. Tipping. Tipping has witnessed many people being cured of incurable diseases and freeing themselves of emotional pain as a result of this process.

Another form of ritual I have found extremely effective is a process that I facilitate by phone, called an Empowerment Session. I've experienced clients' energy fields shift dramatically after releasing personal, and sometimes even ancestral, hatred and unwillingness to forgive. They experience a renewed connection to their source and, as a result, no longer carry the deep tension of spiritual alienation. Invariably their lives open up to a new flow of abundance, and they notice more instances of beauty everywhere around them. They are often able to feel joy in every cell of their bodies for the first time in their lives. As a result, they also experience more love, health and abundance through unexpected channels.

THE BIGGER PICTURE

There is nothing more powerful than your connection with the Source of all of life. So much more than material wealth and success – even more than what you normally perceive as love – can be yours as you awaken to your true self. As you grow in the realization of your true dimensions as a spiritual being, you will experience a bliss beyond imagining.

As your consciousness unfolds, the unlimited universe is able to express ever more of itself through you. The tools you have been given to help you focus on and fully

As you learn to master
your physical reality,
you can begin to trust
that there is a power within you
that is universal and infinite.

manifest the experiences you desire are also stepping stones to experiencing the greater reality of life. Your ideals and your whole identity can expand to include a larger context, for yourself and for the rest of the world.

As you learn to master your physical reality, you can begin to trust that there is a power within you that is universal and infinite. This is the cosmic energy and intelligence out of which everything is created. As you align with it to create ecstasy and success in all areas of your experience, you come to discover that there is a divine purpose to your life, far grander than you might ever before have considered. You begin to live in a new way—and as others join you, a new state of consciousness emerges on the planet.

After experiencing the blissful presence of one of my spiritual teachers, Eckhart Tolle, during many weekend retreats, I became aware of the reality of living in this new way and more convinced that it is available to each of us. As he has often said: "The depth in you is ready." The following words from one of his events made a deep impression on me:

> In the new consciousness, there's a playfulness - and yet a lot of energy flows into it, but it's an energy of play. You play with the world of form...and you realize the whole world of form is a game to be played and enjoyed. You're not dependent on the various forms of life, whether one form stays with you or comes to you or whether it leaves you - it's a game with form, and then that actually becomes quite enjoyable. There's an inner sense of freedom from what you're doing, and yet you're doing it with full care and attention.

The essence of our being is ecstasy,
and when we know who we truly are,
we are no longer caught
in the obsessive quality of the world.

> You don't need any particular outcome anymore because this moment is full enough. There is a fullness of life already. This is a wonderful liberation.

The circumstances of our everyday life need not determine the degree to which we are able to experience ecstasy. Daphne Rose Kingma expressed this beautifully in *The Future of Love*: "We can make the movement to ecstasy a conscious living priority instead of a happy accident."

The essence of our being is ecstasy, and when we know who we truly are, we are no longer caught in the obsessive quality of the world. As we unfold to the joy and playfulness of our true nature, life loses its heaviness, and we recognize our role in the great cosmic dance.

I leave you now with this simple blessing, one that I wish for you and all others on the planet, as expressed through the words of the poet William Blake:

> To see a world in a grain of sand
> And a heaven in a wild flower,
> Hold infinity in the palm of your hand
> And eternity in an hour.

To be guided through the Stillpoint Exercise and Meditation at www.hawaiiheart.com, choose the Keyword: STILLPOINT. To learn Alternate Nostril Breathing, pick the Keyword: BREATH.

INDEX OF TECHNIQUES & EXERCISES

BIBLIOGRAPHY

Chopra, Deepak. *Ageless Body, Timeless Mind.* Three Rivers Press, Reissue edition, 1998.

________. *The Seven Spiritual Laws of Success.* Crown Publishing, 1997.

Emoto, Masaru. *Messages from Water,* Hado (Kyioku Sha) Publishing, Japan, 2000.

Hendricks, Gay and Kathlyn. *Centering and the Art of Intimacy.* Prentice Hall Trade, 1992.

Hill, Napoleon. *Think and Grow Rich.* Fawcett Books, Reissue edition, 1990.

Jwala. *Sacred Sex.* Mandala Books, 1993.

King, Serge Kahili. *Mastering Your Hidden Self.* Theosophical Publishing House, 1985.

Rajneesh, Bhagwan Shree. *Meditation, the First and Last Freedom.* Rebel Publishing House, Reissue edition, 1993.

Roberts, Jane. *The Nature of Personal Reality.* Amber-Allen Publishing, Reprint edition, 1994.

Snow-Davis, Kay. *Point of Power, A Relationship with Your Soul.* Harper Collins (UK), 1995.

Steinem, Gloria. *Marilyn: Norma Jean.* H. Holt & Co., 1986.

Time, Inc. "The Science of Meditation." *Time* (August 4, 2003): Vol. 162, No. 5.

Tolle, Eckhart. *The Power of Now.* Namaste Publishing, 1997.

__________. *Practicing the Power of Now.* New World Library, 1999.

__________. *The Realization of Being.* Audio. Namaste Publishing, 2001. Distributed by Sounds True, Boulder, CO.

ABOUT THE AUTHOR

Kala H. Kos, Ph.D., is the author of *Aloha Power: The Hawaiian Guide to Love, Health and Wealth*, and co-author of *Die Huna-Lehre,* published in Germany, Austria, and Switzerland, and *Moc Aloha I Wiedza Huny*, published in Poland. She has been a freelance writer for more than twenty years.

Trained at the Strasberg School of Acting in New York, Kala performed in theater and film and on television. She also hosted and produced a variety of television shows, including her Los Angeles-based program "From Hawaii With Love". Other productions included a TV pilot with guests Charlie Sheen and Bikram Choudry about Hot Yoga, as well as an environmental documentary entitled "Danger in Paradise", narrated by Graham Nash, which garnered public recognition and acclaim.

While a leader in the human-potential movement, Dr. Kos turned her attention to ancient traditions of self-fulfillment, apprenticing with Serge Kahili King, renowned author and teacher of Hawaiian shamanism. She has studied and taught the Polynesian Huna tradition for nearly two decades and is expert in the application of these practical processes for life transformation. Her Huna workshops are enjoying international acclaim.

Dr. Kos has also studied and taught Tantra, the age-old Indian philosophy and practice of sacred sexuality. Among her teachers were Margo Anand, author of *The Art of Sexual Ecstasy,* Charles and Caroline Muir, who wrote *Tantra: The Art of Conscious Loving*, and Bodhi Avinasha, co-author of *The Jewel in the Lotus.* After trainings in this discipline, she created an ongoing series of "Huna/Tantra" workshops entitled *Ecstasy and Success.*

The founder of the Aloha Empowerment Academy, Kala H. Kos offers a unique program of professional trainings, residential intensives, public workshops, and teleconferencing classes. Dr. Kos did her undergraduate work in Psychology and English Literature at the University of Saskatchewan and the University of Toronto. She received her MA and her Ph.D. in Psychology from Honolulu University. A faculty member and ordained minister with Aloha International, she divides her time between her home bases on the Hawaiian island of Kauai and in British Columbia, Canada.

To Order Books or Audio Recordings by Kala H. Kos
Or Register for Live Events and TeleClasses
Or to Book Speaking Engagements

Visit: www.hawaiiheart.com
Or Call Toll-Free

1-866-GOT-HUNA
1-866-468-4862

BOOKS BY KALA H. KOS, PhD:

Aloha Power
The Hawaiian Guide to Love, Health and Wealth
The 7 Lost Secrets of Ecstasy and Success
How to Awaken Your Hidden Power for Love and Riches

Available in Europe:

Die Huna-Lehre by Kala Kos and John Selby
Published by Wilhelm Goldman Verlag, Munchen
Moc Aloha i Wiedza Huny by Kala Kos and John Selby
Published by Wydawnictwo "KOS," Poland

AUDIO RECORDINGS:

Ecstasy and Success
Power Techniques and Meditations from the Book
The Power of Charisma
How to Become Magnetic to Your Ideal Mate
How to Become a Magnet for Money and Love
Using the 7 Lost Secrets of Ecstasy and Success

LIVE EVENTS:

Ecstasy and Success
Evening Presentation / One-Day Workshop
The Power of Charisma
On-site workshop
The Inner Road to Riches:
Dare to Create Love, Health and Money
On-Site Workshop / Teleclasses
How to See the Invisible and Do the Impossible
On-Site Workshop
Huna: The Art & Science of Manifestation
On-Site Workshop
The Art of Ecstatic Living
Seminar Retreat in Hawaii
Empowerment to the Max – For Trainers
On-Site Workshop

CERTIFICATION TRAINING:

To become a Facilitator of workshops or empowerment sessions, email **trainings@hawaiiheart.com**.

SPEAKING ENGAGEMENTS:

Kala H. Kos is available for lectures, keynote speaker engagements and private consultations.

Aloha Power Publishing

800-15355 24th Avenue
Suite #246
White Rock, B.C.
V4A 2H9 Canada
Fax: 604-535-0249

POB 223204
Princeville, HI
96722 USA
Toll-Free: 866-468-4862

Email: kala@hawaiiheart.com

FOR MORE ECSTASY AND SUCCESS

Step 1 Visit our website at www.hawaiiheart.com. There you can join our Aloha Community by registering for a FREE Aloha Online Newsletter. Each month I'll share with you my thoughts, ideas and practical tools for increasing the love, health and wealth in your life.

Step 2 Register for a FREE teleclass, to join me and people from around the world, in an experiential one-hour program based on the teachings of this book.

Step 3 Attend a FREE group coaching session monthly as a bonus when you purchase my new CD program: How to Become a Magnet for Money and Love, Using the 7 Lost Secrets of Ecstasy and Success.

Step 4 To make a profound shift in your life through the ancient knowledge of Hawaii, attend a seminar in your area. You may wish to become a sponsor in your city or country. Simply send an email to sponsor@hawaiiheart.com. You may even wish to be trained as a facilitator of these seminars. Send an email to trainings@hawaiiheart.com.

I love to hear about your successes and learn through your suggestions. Please send your emails to kala@hawaiiheart.com. Aloha and Many Blessings!

Note: The ancient symbol of the spiral represents our inward journey to self-discovery and our outward striving to unite all that is.

ECSTASY AND SUCCESS ORDER FORM

1. Mail: Aloha Power
   800-15355 24th Ave Suite #246
   White Rock, B.C.
   V4A 2H9 Canada
2. Fax: 604-535-0249. Send this form.
3. Email: orders@hawaiiheart.com
4. Phone: 866-468-4862 for credit card orders.

Name:______________________________

Address;______________________________________

City:__________________Province/State:____________

Zip/Postal/Country Code:_______________

Country:________________E-mail:___________________

Phone:__________________Fax:_____________________

Payment: ❒ Visa ❒ MC ❒ AmEx ❒ Discovery

Credit Card #:____________________________________

Expiration : ____/_____

Signature_________________________________

QTY	PRICE	TOTAL
_____	$14.95 US ($19.95 Cdn)	$___________
	Shipping (see below)	$___________
	TOTAL:	$___________

Shipping and handling charges per book:
$6.00 Within USA
$12.00 Outside USA; $5.00 for each additional